NEIGHBORHOOD CHURCH

Transforming Your Congregation into a Powerhouse for Mission

KRIN VAN TATENHOVE AND ROB MUELLER

WJK WESTMINSTER
JOHN KNOX PRESS
LOUISVILLE · KENTUCKY

First edition
Published by Westminster John Knox Press
Louisville, Kentucky

19 20 21 22 23 24 25 26 27 28—10 9 8 7 6 5 4 3 2 1

Book design by Drew Stevens
Cover design by Mary Ann Smith

Library of Congress Cataloging-in-Publication Data

Names: Van Tatenhove, Krin, author. | Mueller, Robert J., 1934– author.
Title: Neighborhood church : transforming your congregation into a powerhouse
    for mission / by Krin Van Tatenhove and Rob Mueller.
Description: Louisville, KY : Westminster John Knox Press, [2019] | Includes
    bibliographical references. |
Identifiers: LCCN 2018036075 (print) | LCCN 2018052399 (ebook) |
    ISBN 9781611649161 | ISBN 9780664264789 (pbk.)
Subjects: LCSH: Communities—Religious aspects—Christianity. | Evangelistic work.
Classification: LCC BV625 (ebook) | LCC BV625 .V36 2019 (print) |
    DDC 253—dc23
LC record available at https://lccn.loc.gov/2018036075

NEIGHBORHOOD CHURCH

To all those who believe their local church can be a vital sign of God's presence in their community.

—Krin Van Tatenhove

To the members of Divine Redeemer Presbyterian Church and the neighbors of our 78207 zip code who have taught me how to be a pastor.

—Rob Mueller

When Jesus directs us to pray, "Thy kingdom come," he does not mean we should pray for it to come into existence. Rather, we pray for it to take over at all points in the personal, social, and political order where it is now excluded. . . . With this prayer we are invoking it, as in faith we are acting it, into the real world of our daily existence.

—Dallas Willard

Listen with ears of tolerance. See through eyes of compassion. Speak with the language of love.

—Rumi

I want to live where soul meets body.

—Death Cab for Cutie

CONTENTS

INTRODUCTION

December 2, 2016, San Antonio, Texas—a federal judge frees hundreds of women and children from two Texas immigration detention facilities. He has deemed the sites unsuitable for holding minors, sending the families into a wet and frigid winter night.

Members of the San Antonio Mennonite Church, longtime advocates for just immigration, gather to address the emergency. How can they respond to the crisis? What is God calling them to do? Their answer, just one of many stories highlighted in this book, spurred this community of faith further along the path of incarnational mission.

Incarnation, from the Latin *incarnatio,* means "the act of becoming flesh." In various world traditions, it describes the supernatural taking on human form and walking among us. The living lama of Tibet, Vishnu becoming Krishna in Hinduism, or Haile Selassie's status among Rastafarians are vivid examples.

Incarnation reflects the paradox that spirit and flesh can abide in the same place, that we are able to embody the holy in our own lives, and that the material world is precisely where we experience the divine.

When Christians capitalize the word, Incarnation describes the central event of our faith: Jesus of Nazareth personifying God's purposes during his brief life on this planet. In the Gospel of John's poetic prologue, we have this immortal verse, "And the Word became flesh and lived among us . . . full of grace and truth."

What Christians call the Incarnation is certainly not a single act. It is a life-giving metaphor, an invitation to follow for all who will listen. Personally, how can we enflesh the values of love, grace, and justice? As faith communities, how can our collective embodiment of these values shine even brighter? The answers to these questions must always unfold right here, right now, exactly where God has planted us. It will happen *in this place.*

Every Sunday in countless congregations, Christians recite these words from what we call the Lord's Prayer: "Thy kingdom come, thy will be done, on earth as it is in heaven." As we mutter this memorized petition, do we grasp its subversive power? What does it mean? Since Jesus taught this prayer as a model, we turn to him for clarity. His entire ministry was a passionate attempt to illustrate *basileia tou theou*—kingdom of God—as his central metaphor. In one graphic teaching after another, including short stories we call parables, he offers us glimpses of this new reality. It is like

- A father who never stops waiting at the window for his wayward son, and when that son returns, the father celebrates with a sumptuous feast
- A smidgen of yeast that works enormous transformation
- A mustard seed, though tiny, that blooms into a mighty, shade-giving tree

- People who instinctively care for the naked, hungry, imprisoned, or foreigner
- A man who imperils his life and resources to help a stranger of another race, his compassion outweighing prejudice or resentment
- A shepherd so mindful of one missing lamb that he goes on a search-and-rescue mission.

Throughout these teachings, a truth becomes clear. If we want to enter into this kingdom—this new way of being in relationship with God and each other—it requires risk and radical realignment. To say "Thy kingdom come" is a revolutionary confession of willingness.

Many of us long for this revolution to take root in our own lives and communities of faith. Hunger for authenticity crosses generations, as shown in multiple studies describing how Millennials view the church and organized religion. Like many of us, they are tired of the old ABCs of church management: attendance, buildings, cash. Despite a diversity that eludes single catchphrases, common themes shape their approach to mission.

Recently, Austin Presbyterian Theological Seminary uncovered these commonalities by employing a "listener." Rev. Mark Yaconelli spent months hanging out where Millennials hang out, asking questions and deeply listening to their answers. He discovered that Millennials seek a way to incarnate their passions: passion for a just world, passion for a less judgmental church, passion for service that actually makes a difference, passion for a sustainable lifestyle. These desires drive them to act, to incarnate, to take risks by becoming the change they seek for our world.

A good example of Millennial ingenuity is Dr. Matthew Hinsley, whose love of classical guitar and the value of the arts in transforming people's lives led him to create the nonprofit Austin Classical Guitar (ACG). ACG provides guitar classes for over four thousand students in sixty Austin, Texas, schools. Determined to eliminate barriers to accessing the arts, ACG also offers the only daily fine arts class for incarcerated and court-involved youth in Travis County's Juvenile Justice System. Further, they teach a Braille-adapted guitar program at the Texas School for the Blind & Visually Impaired.

Efforts like Hinsley's are filling gaps that the educational and judicial systems have been unable to accomplish. Our failure as a church to capture the imagination, authenticity, and risk-willingness of this generation is crippling our incarnational capacity. It is symptomatic of our reluctance to get messy with the problems of our communities, and to Millennials it communicates a disinterest in real and lasting change.

Pieter Van Tatenhove, age thirty-six, was raised as a preacher's kid, but veered from mainline faith to attend a conservative Christian university. The rigidity he encountered there swung him hard in the opposite direction. One of his last attempts to fit into organized Christianity was with a church plant in northern California. Initially, its core group valued a diversity of opinions, theologies, and political viewpoints. However, when the pastor decided to align himself with a name-brand denomination, the emphasis changed. There was pressure to adhere to a faith statement, and "evangelism" became a numbers game. Though he recently connected with a progressive Episcopal congregation, Pieter had to overcome deep disillusionment. Here he shares some thoughts about his journey:

Most Millennials reject dated definitions of what a 'community of faith' looks like," he says. "We want the church to address its internal hypocrisy, to be more vocal about toxic American Christianity that is not recognizing injustice or loving our neighbors. We are seekers first, Christians second (if at all). We are reluctant to make statements of faith because they calcify that part of our brain that seeks new understanding. For me, the idea of going to church again sounded exhausting. I would rather spend time with my chosen community of seekers, where our common ground is our heart and conscience. Most churches no longer seem relevant.

This book joins hands with others in a quest to kindle new relevancy, especially in a country where Christianity is too often a civic religion, supporting a nationalistic worldview out of sync with biblical admonitions for justice. If we are to change, it will require listening to some painful questions and their prophetic challenges.

Consider questions like those posed by Father Jose Marins, a Brazilian priest who has taught a model of congregational incarnation known as *Comunidades Eclesiales de Base* (Christian Base Communities) since the 1970s. He tells the story of a visit he made to a neighborhood barrio in Los Angeles. It was wracked with violence and disintegration, and yet he observed that there was a church of some kind on nearly every corner. His question to the community was, "Is the church doing anything *at all* about this violence? How can there be so many churches and yet so little transformation?"[1]

Our locales may not be plagued by inner-city ills, but *every* community has its issues. And for many mainline churches, the streets around them have changed dramatically, reflecting shifts in racial and socioeconomic status. It is our calling to incarnate here and now, exactly where we are planted, even if our old neighborhoods look vastly different than they did a few decades ago.

This is the lesson learned by Christian activist and writer Shane Claiborne, who had the privilege of visiting and working with Saint Teresa of Calcutta before her death and canonization. She appreciated the ardor that led him across the globe, but she had an admonition she repeated frequently: "Calcuttas are everywhere if only we have eyes to see. Find your Calcutta."[2]

Her words sound like a simple call to charity. But if we slow down and dig deeper, there's an important, often forgotten piece of Teresa's story. When she asked for permission to leave her religious compound and minister among the denizens of Calcutta, she had no programmatic intention. She set out with two saris and took to the streets. If asked why, she said she could not minister among the poor without truly knowing who they were and how they lived. She later wrote in her diary that her first year was extremely difficult. With no income, she begged for basic necessities, experiencing doubt, loneliness, and a temptation to return to the relatively comfortable life of the convent.

Like historical lodestars, the examples of prophets—past and present—call us further on our pilgrimage. Their clarion message rings true: the realities that Christ responded to so freely are *everywhere* around us. When the walls of our hearts, as well as our churches, become more permeable, we enter into this need and hear the invitation to practice incarnational mission. We leave our comfort, enter a wilderness experience, and out of that dark interval we begin to trust that God will show us how to respond in our given places. We learn to listen, truly listen, remembering Jesus' words, "Those who have ears will hear."

This same journey is reflected in the sea change related to international mission work. The old model of entering a culture with preconceived notions of how to administer justice and convert the populations has thankfully receded in many denominations. The current reality, reflected in the term "coworker," is to discover the best possible ways to join hands with the labor that others and God are already doing. The key is dialogue. As Paulo Freire so brilliantly said, "Leaders who do not act dialogically, but insist on imposing their decisions, do not organize the people—they manipulate them. They do not liberate, nor are they liberated: they oppress."[3]

In his popular, prophetic book *Toxic Charity: How Churches and Charities Hurt Those They Help (And How to Reverse It)*, Robert Ludlum iconoclastically tears down cherished models of service. It is a must-read for anyone intent on incarnational mission. His basic premise is that most of what passes for ministry fosters dependency, ruptures authentic relationships, and squanders valuable resources. Essentially, this "old wineskin" mind-set is disempowering to those on the "receiving" end.

Ludlum says, "Giving to those in need what they could be gaining from their own initiative may well be the kindest way to destroy people."[4] He believes there is no real way to discern a proper response without relationships.

In the pages ahead, you will find practical tools for developing these incarnational relationships. Though this is certainly—and primarily—a spiritual journey, it draws essential wisdom from the field of community organizing, specifically the power of asset-based community development (ABCD). This method of partnering with others first came to light in 1993 at the Institute for Policy Research, Northwestern University, Evanston, Illinois. Its seemingly simple approach is Copernican in effect. Rather than focusing on deficiencies and weaknesses, ABCD highlights and amplifies the gifts of individuals as well as organizations within a community. It stimulates an incarnational mind-set, starting with what is present and building on these strengths.

ABCD helps congregations cultivate connections within their communities, mobilizing the capacities of everyone involved to produce change from within. One of its key concepts is to move from a "fixed sum dynamic to an open sum dynamic," meaning that true partnership discovers and stimulates benefits for *everyone* involved.

Thankfully, others have blazed new trails before us, men and women engaged in new models of mission. You will meet many of them in these pages. You will hear the stories of their joys and struggles as they minister in their settings.

We (Krin and Rob) have over sixty years of combined experience working with congregations in challenging environments. It has been a great privilege, and we share some of our personal stories in this book, found as sidebars to the narrative flow. Our work has been difficult, but the thrill of seeing the kingdom become visible in small and large ways is incomparable. The chapters ahead outline five critical practices we have discerned over the years: (1) converting our perspective from scarcity to abundance, and from self-absorption to our neighbors; (2) learning to listen as an essential discipline; (3) embracing transformative partnership; (4) integrating our buildings in new ways; and (5) sustaining our vision, especially through Spirit-filled worship and the mentoring of new leaders.

We hope that the concepts and stories you encounter here will help you incarnate God's love and grace right here, right now. *In this place . . .*

Chapter 1
COMMUNAL CONVERSION

It is impossible to be truly converted to God without
being converted to our neighbor.
—John R. W. Stott

Though it may be a dramatic demarcation line, conversion
is never a onetime event. It is a perpetual process—a shed-
ding of soul skins—as we grow into stronger, more flexible
spirituality. When conversion means adopting a fundamental set of principles, and then wielding them defensively in
our commerce with others, the results can be tragic. We
have all seen this in practice. Social media thrives on con-
tention, with true believers slinging opinions and invectives
at each other over a myriad of issues. If we extricate our
egos from the stream of debate, we see how much of it ends
up dividing us rather than promoting unity.

Ongoing conversion is an antidote to this cancerous
inflexibility. James Fowler, in his landmark work on stages
of faith, talked about the critical evolution from Stage Three
to Stage Four. He called it a movement from "Synthetic-
Conventional Faith" to "Individuative-Reflective Faith."
It happens when we are willing to question the beliefs we
inherited from our dominant culture or family. We awaken
to healthy doubts about our cherished convictions. We
begin to examine, without censorship, the worldviews of
others. We question authority, and it can be a fearful and
risky experience. As Fowler said, "When we are grasped
by the vision of a center of value and power more luminous,
more inclusive and more true than that to which we are

9

devoted, we initially experience the new as the enemy or the slayer—that which destroys our 'god.'"[1]

If we stay the course, we find the beauties inherent in Stages Five and Six. This is when we recognize the limits of logic and start to accept paradoxes. We begin to see life as a mystery. We often return to sacred stories and symbols, but this time without confinement to a theological or ideological box. We relish the diversity of myths and symbols in our world, gleaning what they teach us with an open mind. Not enough people reach this stage. Many who reach this stage find their deepest meaning in the service of others.

What is true for individuals is also true for our communities of faith. Our experience is that congregations can have "communal conversions." This change is a turning, a revolving away from ourselves and toward the streets where God has planted us. Just as individuals learn to open their sealed mind-sets to the light of new truths, congregations can learn to embrace fundamental changes in perspective.

Two aspects of this transformation are essential: *conversion from scarcity to abundance* and *conversion to our neighbors*.

CONVERSION FROM SCARCITY TO ABUNDANCE

During times of stress and challenge, congregations often pull inside themselves like hermit crabs into a borrowed shell. This can be a reaction to internal conflict, radically changing neighborhoods, or fear about the fate of our denomination. This survival mentality flows from an outlook of scarcity. Old ways of doing ministry are no longer adequate, but there is no imagining of something different. Finances may be historically low, and no one proposes a scenario to turn things around. The same leaders cycle through petrified volunteer positions until they are bone-tired, without recognizing the gifts and potential of others.

A conversion from paucity to plenty must begin in the hearts and minds of each member. Rooted in the soil of gratitude for our faith and calling, it grows into new hope and vision.

What are the tools for this transformation? Take your pick! There are numerous books, small group studies, and meditations about the power of positive thinking. Often dismissed by the jaded or cynical, they nonetheless provide basic building blocks for fresh optimism. Central to this popular literature is a clear premise: gratitude for "what is" demands disciplined attention, a daily recounting of the many blessings our Creator showers on us.

How many of us sagaciously nod our heads as we hear Jesus say, "Do not worry! Which one of you by worrying can add a single hour to your life?" Then, in the fray of daily living, how often do we allow fear to cloud our lives? Many of us believe that nurturing an outlook of abundance is key to self-actualization, but when faced with daunting challenges, how often do we revert to notions of scarcity for ourselves, our families, our congregations?

> **Krin:** As a recovering alcoholic, I believe that followers of Christ can learn a lot from the recovery community. Imbedded in our literature is the concept that gratitude is the lifeblood of a growing spirituality. Putting down our addictions, though essential, is just the first step. The hard work, the *bulk* of the work, has to do with changing our self-destructive personality traits and the thoughts that fueled them.

My friends and I agree that ours is not primarily a drinking problem, but a thinking problem. As our literature says, "An honest regret for harms done, a genuine *gratitude* for blessings received, and a willingness to try for better things tomorrow will be the permanent assets we shall seek."[2] Addicts and alcoholics know that thankfulness is as necessary as air for our continued recovery. We call this "working our program," and we know that daily discipline provides a reprieve from the "stinking thinking" we allowed to dominate our lives for so long.

It is not a stretch to say that the same is true for congregations desiring new vitality of mission. Their corporate self-conceptions, their theologies, their beliefs about their pasts and futures, *all* of these require a conversion from scarcity to abundance. We stand on the shoulders of giants who have embraced this process. Hebrew and Christian Scriptures brim with joyous optimism. Consider the witness of the Apostle Paul, whose ongoing conversion gave us words like these:

> Finally, beloved, whatever is true, whatever is honorable, whatever is just, whatever is pure, whatever is pleasing, whatever is commendable, if there is any excellence and if there is anything worthy of praise, think about these things.
>
> Philippians 4:8

> I am confident of this, that the one who began a good work among you will bring it to completion.
>
> Philippians 1:6a

For no matter how many promises God has made, they are "Yes" in Christ.

2 Corinthians 1:20a (NIV)

For such words and attitudes to become part of a congregation's DNA, we need visible champions of positivity, vibrant encouragers whose enthusiasm functions like the yeast in Jesus' parable, working its way through our community of faith.

This encourager can be you! To put it more bluntly, if you desire incarnational mission for your congregation— but are still held captive by limited thinking—you are part of the problem rather than the solution.

> **Krin:** I remember Janet, an elder at a church I served on the edge of Los Angeles County. What an encourager! God had imbued her with indefatigable optimism and the spiritual gift of exhortation. Whenever any of us began to negatively focus on our deficiencies rather than our blessings, she would blurt out, "Crop failure!" Once you got beyond the seeming rudeness of her interruption—usually with a single glance at her winsome smile—her simple but profound message sank in: we reap what we sow!
>
> That congregation was poor, situated in a lonely stretch of the high desert, but its dirt parking lot and faded chapel belied the vibrant conversion taking place at the heart of its membership. It was growing rapidly as a multigenerational, multiracial powerhouse of mission. This growth, like any, was sometimes uncomfortable, even painful, taxing available resources. It was tempting for some of us to lapse

into a perspective of scarcity. At those key moments, Janet would inevitably remind us of crop failure!

I recall a particular challenge we faced. Our swelling educational program was outstripping available space in our facility. By then, a can-do attitude, fueled by cheerleaders like Janet, had become the norm. We bought used wooden sheds, refurbished them with the help of congregational carpenters, added window AC units, then lined the finished structures along a gravel pathway in the back. It wasn't pretty, but it was functional.

I was standing there one Sunday morning with Janet, listening to the hum of voices engaged with each other and Scripture. She turned to me and said, "Now, that's a harvest!"

In his popular book *Five Practices of Fruitful Congregations*, Robert Schnase talks extensively about the inner paradigm shift necessary for what he calls "extravagant generosity" to flow from a community of faith.

"Vibrant, fruitful, growing congregations practice extravagant generosity," he says. "They thrive with the joy of abundance rather than starve with a fear of scarcity. They give joyously, generously, and consistently in ways that enrich the souls of members and strengthen the ministries of the church."[3]

Congregations and their leaders who hope to convert from scarcity to abundance must be intentional in offering pathways to this new reality. First and foremost is a call for all church leaders to examine their own visions for ministry. This requires personal soul-searching and courageous receptivity to the feedback of others. We ask ourselves these penetrating questions. Am I modeling abundant optimism?

Is my personal viewpoint a part of the joyful and contagious vision our leadership has adopted as its mission statement? If not, will I commit to the spiritual disciplines—including counseling and mentoring—that will help me grow?

The next step is to lead the congregation as a whole. We can offer worship experiences like those outlined in *The Abundance of God* by Rev. Erica Schemper, a minister in the Presbyterian Church (U.S.A.). With a theology focused on Creation's goodness rather than "the Fall," she leads us from Genesis to Revelation, showing how biblical narratives spill over with an abundance of beauty, grace, and hope. The consistent theme is that God has provided more than enough for our needs and the needs of our neighbors if we learn to share extravagantly.

"One of the strengths of this approach," says Schemper, "is that it doesn't . . . push us to a form of asceticism that is at odds with a Christian outlook that celebrates the goodness of the physical creation. Instead, it's rooted in the idea that creation is good, God is gracious to the point of overflow, and we can work to ensure that everyone has what they need to thrive."[4]

How critical is this conversion? Listen to these words by Walter Brueggemann from his essay "The Liturgy of Abundance, the Myth of Scarcity." He decries what he calls the "demonic force" of consumerism that continues to reinforce fears of scarcity:

> The conflict between the narratives of abundance and of scarcity is the defining problem confronting us at the turn of the millennium. The Gospel story of abundance asserts that we originated in the magnificent, inexplicable love of a God who loved the world into generous being. The baptismal service

declares that each of us has been miraculously loved into existence by God. And the story of abundance says that our lives will end in God, and that this well-being cannot be taken from us. In the words of Saint Paul, neither life nor death nor angels nor principalities nor things—nothing can separate us from God. What we know about our beginnings and our endings, then, creates a different kind of present tense for us. We can live according to an ethic whereby we are not driven, controlled, anxious, frantic or greedy, precisely because we are sufficiently at home and at peace to care about others as we have been cared for.[5]

Reclaiming this recognition of abundance is also at the heart of asset-based community development. Its practitioners guide people through asset-mapping workshops. The purpose is to help them concentrate deeply on the resources already alive and present in individuals, their organization, and the wider community.

Suzy Yowell is director of the Growing Field, a nonprofit that focuses on building the capacity of historic sacred places. Their goal is to see churches, synagogues, and mosques better serve their communities as anchor institutions. They help these places restore their buildings *and* engage their neighborhoods in new and powerful ways.

Yowell embraces asset mapping wholeheartedly:

I believe it is the most valuable thinking tool a congregation can have. Identifying and mapping the strengths of your members, your building, and your community encourages and inspires your congregation. It empowers you to take action. It is too easy to get into the habit of thinking from a needs-based place when we are dealing with the everyday challenges of worn buildings, diminishing memberships, disconnection from our community. Asset mapping can break this paralyzing cycle. We stop dwelling on what we don't have and start focusing on what we *do* have. We begin to see a clear picture of how we can connect our many strengths and build upon them. As a result, we completely change our direction and drive. I've seen amazing transformation arise from this simple yet powerful shift in perspective.

Yowell can point to many "aha" moments as congregants awakened to their value in a variety of ways. They found exciting possibilities for deploying their assets:

- Ample green space converted to community gardens, dog parks, and places for meditation
- Fellowship halls with performance stages now used by nonprofit theater companies raising up young actors
- Underused gymnasiums now resounding with the voices of community sports leagues and charter schools
- Dormant classrooms now providing program space for a county's service to developmentally delayed children and their parents
- Office spaces converted to nonprofit incubators for their communities

In these cases and many others, new connections are just the beginning. Our belief is that churches must also move from simple repurposing to what we call "integrating our space," a distinction we will talk about thoroughly in chapter 4.

More and more congregations are contracting with consultants who conduct asset-mapping workshops. These can be stand-alone events or woven into weekend leadership retreats. In Appendices 1 and 4, you will find the outline for an asset-mapping workshop, as well as a list of individuals and organizations that are experts in this field. Investing in their services is a bold move that will pay lasting dividends for the life of a congregation intent on converting to abundance.

CONVERSION TO OUR NEIGHBORS

If our Christian conviction regarding incarnation teaches us anything, it is this: the world we live in is the place where we encounter God. As Paula D'Arcey says, "God comes disguised as our life."[6] Consequently, the neighborhoods where we abide are places of revelation where we encounter God if we are paying attention. We are all raised with a set of lenses that both focuses and obscures the presence of God. Looking for signs of life amid the signs that oppose life is a discipline we must cultivate. For instance, when one comes from a social class that enjoys privilege, it is easy to miss the gifts that are present in the midst of an impoverished neighborhood.

This begins with personal conversions from our own racism, sexism, classism, and homophobia, discovering our common humanity, the image and likeness of God within all of us. Once we perceive this, then "the other" becomes our teacher, capable of revealing an aspect of God that no one else could unveil.

Rob: For me, embracing incarnation means embracing the very messiness of life and expecting God to be there. As I encounter my alcoholic neighbor repeatedly and learn to honestly admit my disgust, judgment, and disdain for her, I become aware of my limitations in extending divine grace. When I work on the dilapidated roof of a filthy home inhabited by a man and his mother who, for various reasons, will never be capable of cleaning it, it challenges me to ask myself, "So, Rob, does the grace of our community service extend only to the nice and neat neighbors? Must someone *earn* our good work on their behalf, or is it genuinely grace, given freely and without a *holiness or purity requirement?*" I must wrestle with a God whose mercy and love shine equally upon those considered unclean. I must have an open heart to learn the lessons God is offering.

Neighborhoods teach us these same lessons. Each of them has particular gifts that provide unique opportunities to encounter the holy tangled up with other, unholy realities. In some places, these unholy aspects are poverty and violence that put residents at risk, especially children and youth. In other places, the darker truths are apathy, indifference, racism, and classism. Yet, in *every* locale, there also exist the gifts and insights that make it possible to experience incarnation.

Who needs whom? This is the critical question. Often, we do mission with the perception that those on the receiving end are the ones in need. The truth, however, is that those most in need of conversion are often the givers—those whose privilege and position prevent them from seeing the reality that others experience, and the grace with which they engage it. We are the ones trapped in our towers of theological and social purity, the contemporary equivalents of the keepers of the Law and the purity codes in Jesus' time.

Unless we become capable of a poverty of spirit, recognizing the need that inhabits our plenty, we remain blind. Unless we learn to identify the gifts of a community and not simply its liabilities, we remain blind. Unless we discover that we have *at least* as much to learn as we have to teach, we remain blind, unable to possess the kingdom that Jesus promised to the poor in spirit.

Can we see ourselves as partners in the ministry God is already performing around us? Are we willing to include the voices of our neighbors in the decisions of our churches? In his book *Radical Outreach: The Recovery of Apostolic Ministry and Evangelism*, George Hunter poses critical questions for congregations to consider. Each one progressively challenges our willingness to convert to our neighbors. Do we really want to know them? Are we willing to go where they are? Are we willing to be in genuine relationship with them? Are we willing for our church to become their church? Will we allow them to have a say in the decisions of our church's future? Will we stand with them and experience the life they are experiencing?[7]

> **Rob:** About a month before writing these pages, I unexpectedly became a material witness to a homicide that occurred on the front porch of a home opposite our church property. This home is notorious for

dealing drugs. Our church's neighbors and I have regularly lamented the presence and negative impact that it and other drug-dealing homes have on our community, especially our youth. Though we share this frustration, we have been stymied on how to address it. Neighbors were afraid of retribution if they reported anything, so they kept silent. The majority of the illegal activity occurs in the evenings, but when twelve shots rang out on at 10:00 a.m. on a Tuesday morning as 100 people stood in line to receive emergency food support, we were all stunned.

I had heard stories, listened to neighbors' descriptions of other shooting incidents, and talked with youth about the pressure to join gangs, but when I became a witness to the death of another person, something flipped in me. I could no longer stay at the sidelines. I had to figure out how to stop this.

But it is not easy to identify solutions. While giving my statement to the police, I began to feel fearful questions creeping into my consciousness. What if they ambush me late at night when I'm leaving church? What if they target the church itself in some kind of attack? I could feel this fear reach its sticky tentacles into my former resolve to act. It was at that moment that I recognized, "This is how my neighbors feel *all the time*!" They are afraid to act because they are afraid to be targeted, and yet we *have* to figure out how to work together on this.

I began to converse with neighbors about the drug activity in our area. They know the players, what they sell, when they sell it, and who is buying. But they can't speak up. I didn't have that information, but I could speak up. I was already compromised, so why stop now? We began the process of engagement with local authorities—a panorama of resources we didn't even know existed (unexpected abundance) including the fire department, code compliance, county taxing authorities, the local police department and more. Our strategy has been to collect information via neighbors, channel it through the church to protect the community, and slowly and deliberately, one by one, remove the dealers from our area. A sense of hope is rising, the prospect of a future where the children of our community will not have to resist appeals to buy or sell contraband or be bullied. We are feeling our power together as we have now shut down four of the five drug-dealing locations.

What made the difference was a willingness to personally experience the anger, pain, and paralysis of my neighbors. I had to dive into the depths of their reality, a conversion to their experience, so that together we could find the available abundance that would make it possible to address an overwhelming deficit.

Rev. Mike Mather, senior pastor of Broadway United Methodist Church (BUMC), Indianapolis, is a frequent presenter at ABCD training events. Both he and his congregation have been on a long journey of embracing its core principles, a pilgrimage he highlights in his recent book called *Having Nothing, Possessing Everything: Finding Abundant Communities in Unexpected Places.*

Mather often utters prophetic phrases meant to wake people up from their normal paradigm of doing ministry. In an article published in *Faith and Leadership*, he remarked, "One of the things we literally say around here is 'Stop helping people!' I'm serious. The church, and me in particular, have done a lot of work where we treated the people around us as if, at worst, they are a different species, and at best, as if they are people to be pitied and helped by us."[8]

Instead of defining their urban Indianapolis neighborhood in terms of its needs and deficiencies, BUMC decided that its calling was to simply be a good neighbor. The first step in this conversion has been learning to listen, discovering the depths of assets that are all around them, something we will discuss further in the next chapter.

The result has been radical when it comes to BUMC's traditional ministries. Gone are the food pantry, clothing ministry, and after-school program. When people ask, "How can I get involved?" the church answers, "We want to know how *we* can get involved with *you*. What do you care about, or give yourself to, in this world? Can we share it with others? Are there ways others can be involved with you?"

Can you hear the conversion happening?

Like many churches, BUMC includes a "Who We Are" section on its website. We quote it here because it aligns beautifully with the principles contained in this book.

WE ARE A JOYOUS COMMUNITY. We believe life is to be joyous, even in the midst of sorrow and pain. In our life together, we celebrate one another's milestones, successes, and ministries as well as honoring the ministries that have come to an end. In worship, we lift up our concerns to God as well as "pass the peace" to the entire congregation!

WE SEE ABUNDANCE. We believe everybody is a child of God with gifts to offer the world. But society often overlooks these gifts, seeing only labels and categories, needs, and stereotypes. Our church is located in a low-income community and our congregation comes from a variety of experiences and backgrounds, but we strive to focus on the many, diverse gifts of our neighbors and members, not their deficiencies.

WE "HAVE CONVERSATIONS AND HAVE FAITH." We believe that the Spirit of God is alive in all people. We welcome persons of all age, race, ethnicity, gender identity or sexual orientation. We seek to acknowledge and honor this spirit in all people by having conversations and listening for opportunities to connect and invest in the passions, interests, and gifts they have to share with the world.

WE BELIEVE IN EXTRAVAGANT GRACE. We believe that God loves us all, and nothing we do—or don't do—can change that. God's grace has been revealed to us in Jesus, who came to give abundant life, to restore sight to the blind, to heal the sick and brokenhearted, to proclaim good news to the poor, and to release the oppressed.[9]

CASE STUDY: SAN ANTONIO MENNONITE CHURCH, SAN ANTONIO, TEXAS

Let's return to that frigid December night in 2016 that we mentioned in the first paragraph of the Introduction, a time when scores of immigrant women and children found themselves on the streets. The San Antonio Mennonite Church (SAMC) acted in a powerful way, a response that arose from their unique history.

This urban congregation purchased the building of San Antonio's old Westminster Presbyterian Church in the mid-1980s, a Mediterranean-style structure listed as a land-mark by San Antonio's Office of Historic Preservation. It sits on a main artery that connects downtown to the famous sixteenth-century missions on the south side. A few years later, at some sacrifice, the congregation also purchased a large two-story guest house on the edge of what is known as the King William District.

Mennonites have a long tradition of social justice engagement. Their theology calls for reconciliation and nonviolence in the midst of whatever culture God plants them. In keeping with this tradition, SAMC has opened its buildings to numerous nonprofits that counter domestic violence, minister to people struggling with addictions, educate children, and advocate for immigrants.

In 2014, waves of Central American refugees flooded the South Texas border. Women with their children, as well as unaccompanied minors, were fleeing cartel-induced violence in their home countries, many of them fearing for their lives. The U.S. government contracted with a for-profit prison company to establish and maintain two detention facilities in South Texas for the immigrants.

These women and children required legal counsel as they applied for asylum status, and if they obtained the right to stay with family members in the U.S., they also needed support for overnight housing, transportation, and basic necessities in the gap between their release from detention and their departure to be united with loved ones.

About the same time of this mass migration, a nonprofit operating out of SAMC's guest house closed, leaving the church with open space begging for new purpose. The congregation decided to use it as a center for assisting refugees. Their decision was born of a theological conviction that these refugees are neighbors—brothers and sisters in the family of God. The church partnered with the Refugee and Immigrant Center for Education and Legal Services, a nonprofit that provides free and low-cost legal services to immigrants and refugees, as well as the Interfaith Welcome Coalition, a consortium of churches dedicated to the same purposes.

With additional help from volunteers among the church's membership, this new partnership proved fruitful. Anywhere from eight to one hundred individuals came through the center daily. It was an orderly, manageable, ongoing ministry that was mostly under the radar.

That is, until December 2016 . . .

As officials released women and children from two detention facilities in response to a court order, hundreds of people suddenly needed temporary shelter and support. On Friday, December 2, 2016, SAMC's leadership offered its guest house as a shelter. When its two floors filled up, they opened their cavernous fellowship hall, and when even that area overflowed, they opened the doors of their main sanctuary, pushing pews to the walls to provide sleeping space.

At the guest house, a big-screen TV hung from the ceiling announcing departure times for women and children bound for destinations around the U.S. Upstairs was a phone bank for calling lawyers and family members, its long line extending into the hallway.

Immigration and Customs Enforcement (ICE) learned of SAMC's willingness to shelter the released prisoners and began to bus them directly to the church's front steps. Their numbers continued to swell.

John Garland, pastor of SAMC, reflects on that experience and how its ripple effects continue to shape the congregation's ministry.

"It's easy," he says, "to quote Old and New Testament mandates to care for the least and the aliens in our midst. But real conversion to our neighbors doesn't begin by declaring ourselves a welcoming space for the homeless or a sanctuary for refugees. It *always* begins in real, face-to-face relationships. This is the essence of incarnational ministry."

Garland, like most of SAMC's members, was at the eye of that human hurricane for a number of days. The experience reaffirmed many of the congregation's cherished beliefs. For instance, Mennonites strive to live simply, believing God will provide more than we need as we walk the path of faithfulness. This trust in abundance proved warranted during the refugee crisis in a number of ways.

Hundreds of surrounding neighbors rose up to provide support in the way of food, water, and backpacks for the traveling women. Many of them openly said, "I don't believe in God, but I'm glad you are here and I support what you are doing."

When the fire marshal got wind of the church's overcrowded conditions, he threatened to shut everything down. This evoked responses from the mayor, the city council, even a congressional representative, all of them wrangling over what to do. But it was the neighborhood fire station that provided the solution. Its firemen, even after working long shifts, volunteered to patrol the perimeter of the church, providing the emergency coverage necessary to make everything legal.

Not everyone, however, was approving of SAMC's work. Online threats were frequent, some of them warning of violence, and though Pastor Garland never read the specifics, he was aware of potential danger. So, when a jacked-up truck with a Confederate flag on its rear window rumbled into the parking lot, he was understandably concerned. A burly man stepped down from the cab.

"Is this the place that's helping the illegals?" he asked in a gruff voice.

"Yes, it is," said Garland.

"Good," said the man, "because I have some food in the back I'd like to donate to the cause."

Garland sees this not only as an example of the abundant response of others, but of the unlikely conversion of one neighbor to another in our midst.

There is another incident dear to his heart. During that onslaught of need, SAMC discovered a child separated from his mother. In all the hubbub, some volunteers had taken the mother to the hospital. Until they located her, Garland took the child home and let him snuggle between his two young daughters, a lasting lesson for him and his girls about the need to protect and love our neighbors no matter how they come to us.

He sums up so much of what he learned in a succinct anecdote.

"On the fullest night of that crisis, with the church packed, I tried to sleep in my office. The building was a cacophony of two primary noises. There was the beeping of the ankle monitors each detainee was required to wear, and the coughing! Most of the women had caught a respiratory bug in the detention facilities, and the coughing was nonstop. Between those signs of sickness and the incessant beeping, I thought I was going to lose my mind.

"Then a beautiful voice rose above the din. It was a mother singing a lullaby to her child. That song had a clear message to me. 'Sorry, white boy, if you are struggling this evening, but I'm trying to put my child to sleep.'

"I realized right then that none of us responding to this crisis were the heroes in this passion play. It was these women who had left everything—their homes, their countries of origin—to protect their children."

The overcrowded conditions eventually subsided, but not the regular and ongoing need. Today, SAMC and its partners continue to minister to the women and children who come to them from the detention facilities—these neighbors in a global family—but now their service echoes with an even deeper connection born of those days in December 2016.

DISCUSSION STARTERS

1. Have you had a conversion in your life, or have your witnessed one in others? If so, describe the experience.
2. Do you personally have an outlook of abundance? If not, what is blocking you from this perspective?
3. Consider your congregation's life together. Have you embraced an abundant mind-set, a sense that there is more than enough and that with God all things are possible? Or is the prevailing mood one of survival, a fear of shrinking resources and possibilities?
4. What assets does your congregation have that may be underutilized and unappreciated?
5. What kind of person do you find it hardest to accept?
6. When it comes to true diversity—welcoming and incorporating people across cultural and economic lines—how would you describe your congregation?

PRAYER

Loving God, as we dwell upon the abundant goodness you have provided for us, we say, "Thank you." We vow to cherish the wealth of your gifts to us: life, breath, loving, and sharing. For all these things, including the abundance we are still discovering around us, we give you praise. Amen.

Chapter 2
THE DNA OF LISTENING

It is no longer a question of a Christian going about to
convert others to the faith, but of each one being ready
to listen to the other and so to grow together in mutual
understanding.
—Bede Griffiths

Paul Tillich famously said, "The first duty of love is to listen." No matter how many times we hear these words, their
truth remains profound. Before we focus on the impact
listening can have on our congregations, let's plumb the
deeper meaning of this art.

THE ALTAR OF OUR EARS

We begin our lives hearing sounds in the womb. On our
deathbeds, hearing is the last sense to fade. In our allotted
days—that dash between our dates—we have myriad opportunities to listen. Our world brims with inspiring messages
if we cultivate the practices of attention and openness. W.
A. Mathieu, a Sufi musician from Northern California,
describes these disciplines as "making an altar of our ears."

In America, however, it seems we are losing both our
ability and desire to listen. We know how to take polarized
sides and argue. We know how to quickly respond with
labels, categories, and our own entrenched opinions. We
know how to watch, plugged into devices and screens of
varying sizes, some of us from infancy. Yes, we will watch,

maybe even listen, as long as the content is quick and to the point!

However, if we listen from a perspective of abundance rather than scarcity, we can discern subtle shifts in our nation's climate. There is growing evidence that people are slowing down and paying more attention to the world around them.

We see this in the popular fascination with "mindfulness," a moment-by-moment awareness of our thoughts, feelings, bodily sensations, and environment. Rooted in Eastern meditation practices, especially those of Buddhism, it is more than just awareness. It emphasizes acceptance, being conscious of the streaming thoughts and feelings that flit across our minds without immediately judging them as bad or good. Mindfulness cultivates a dispassionate observation of reality before we spring into action.

Fourth Presbyterian Church, Chicago, offers a range of classes on mindfulness and contemplation through its Replogle Center for Counseling and Well-Being. These include Sacred Pause—twenty minutes of contemplative prayer in silence—as well as an evening meditation called Silence in Community. They have a Labyrinth Ministry with docent-hosted walks, and they sponsor trips to spiritual "thin places" like Iona, Scotland.

Marsha Heizer, a member of Fourth Church, has joined these activities as both a recipient and leader. "The experience has been transformative," she says, "expanding and deepening my journey of faith. It has been like the blossoming of a beautiful flower that sinks its roots into the rich loam of God's deep, everlasting, and unconditional love. Most importantly, I have opened myself to listening for God's still, small voice that allows me to grow in this love."

This attention to the present is needed in our ministries. It opens our ears to the treasure-filled stories of those in our neighborhoods, trusting that they hold the exact lessons we need to hear. Listening like this is sacred, the foundation of our struggles for peace and justice. It is incarnational practice at its most basic level, and sometimes we have to learn it from people of other faiths and cultures.

Krin: I once got "schooled" about listening from a Navajo neighbor while living in New Mexico. We would occasionally sit and converse on the common walkway of our apartment building. I tend to be extremely verbal, and after sharing my animated thoughts, I noticed something strange. I would stop my monologue and wait for a response. The only reaction I got was open eyes, a wide smile, and silence. At first, I had some uncharitable thoughts. Maybe the lights were on but nobody was home. Perhaps he needed to get out and socialize more often.

Yet, if I remained silent in the awkward pause, he would finally respond with words that were often wise and precise. He explained to me that this is a Navajo custom. Before speaking, and especially after listening, they let blessed silence permeate the present. This allows the other person to add or subtract from their message. It is a sign of respect, and even more importantly, an effort to make sure that they have heard the whole story before responding or acting. Navajos believe listening is a sacred part of *hozho*, being in harmony with the world and others.

Rev. Kay Lindahl, author and founder of the Listening Center in Long Beach, California, has dedicated her life to training others in the sacred art of listening. She says, "The cultural and religious diversity of our communities calls for a way of listening that transcends words and belief systems. Learning to truly listen to one another is the beginning of new understanding and compassion, which deepens and broadens our sense of community."[1]

Another cultural sign of our renewed interest in listening is StoryCorps, a national effort to record and preserve America's oral history. Since its founding in 2003 with a StoryBooth in New York City's Grand Central Terminal, this nonprofit has enjoyed widespread success. StoryCorps echoes efforts of the Works Progress Administration of the 1930s, which archived oral history interviews across America. Another inspiration is the oral historian Studs Turkel, whose works like *The Good War* and *Working* mined the wealth of everyday realities surrounding us. To date, StoryCorps has recorded more than sixty thousand interviews in all fifty states, Washington, D.C., and several American territories.

Dave Isay, editor of StoryCorps's first collection of interviews, speaks about the movement's principles. Imagine how these same values could shape the hearts and minds of every member in our congregations.

> StoryCorps is built on a few basic ideas. . . . That our stories—the stories of everyday people—are as important as the celebrity stories we're bombarded with by the media every minute of the day. That if we take the time to listen, we'll find wisdom, wonder, and poetry in the lives and stories of the people all around us. That we all want to know that our lives have mattered and we won't be forgotten. That listening is an act of love.[2]

This core vision resonates with *Dare to Listen,* a joint project of Texas Public Radio, the San Antonio Area Foundation, and the John L. Santikos Charitable Foundation. It boldly suggests a special focus in our divided country—inviting participants to intentionally seek out others with opposing viewpoints. The effort's website powerfully captures the current deafness in America through these simple words:

> We all feel it. This is a time of collective frustration. This impasse of angry proportion. We are all living it. And we are all diminished by it. This is not who we are. We are a nation founded upon the very idea of tolerance. How did we get here? Somewhere along the way we let go of each other's hands. We stopped creating connections and started severing ties. Today we are a nation with our hands over our ears. Have we become afraid to listen? To listen is risky. Because when we truly listen, we might just change our minds. To listen is risky. But to not listen is riskier. We believe it's time to consider, think, explore, and question. To appreciate our differences and find our commonalities. To reach across the fence, build the bridge, open our minds. To talk. And most of all, listen.[3]

LISTENING IN OUR CHURCHES

Of all institutions, the church should be leading the effort to listen attentively to others. This is a holy gift we offer to our communities in an era of rancorous social discourse. We have a powerful example in Jesus, who modeled listening at so many junctures in his ministry:

- The moments he spent with a Samaritan woman at Jacob's Well, overcoming barriers and taboos that existed in both their tribes (John 4:1–26)
- His heartfelt response to the searching of the rich young ruler, reflected in a single verse, "Jesus, looking at him, loved him" (Mark 10:21a)
- His late-night repartee with Nicodemus, a ruling member of the Sanhedrin who was intrigued by the Nazarene's teachings (John 3:1–21)
- His attentiveness to his disciples after he asked them the question, "Who do people say that the Son of Man is?" (Matt. 16:13–20)
- His urgency in calling us to hear his words about the kingdom of God, saying, "Let anyone with ears to hear listen!" (Matt. 4:21–25)

If we are going to model the example of Jesus, what are some practical ways we can weave listening into our congregations? How can we make it part of our collective DNA?

We can begin by hearing Scripture with new depth and attentiveness. Conservative churches that espouse the inerrancy of the Bible rarely question its literal truth. Many Christians in the Reformed tradition have a far different paradigm. Modern forms of biblical criticism, as well as scholarship by the likes of the Jesus Seminar, have shaped our awareness of both the Bible's veracity *and* limitations.

However, it is important not to let our modern mentality cloud our appreciation of holy texts. Scripture still breathes, and we can listen to its whisperings and bold proclamations on multiple levels. In churches that are experiencing revival, you will often find a growing awareness that the Bible is alive to us in the present, not just confined to historical annals. This is why the ancient Benedictine practice of *lectio divina* continues to gain recognition and popularity. Adam S. McHugh points to this in his book *The Listening Life*:

> The practice of *lectio divina* is what resurrected my devotional reading of the Bible. It takes the Bible's inspiration so seriously that it declares every word, every letter and every squiggle has its ultimate origin in God. Those words and characters are not stuck in the past but, because they are enlivened by the Holy Spirit, are means for God's communication with us today. Lectio listens through old words for a new word.[4]

We can utilize *lectio divina*, or modified versions, when we read Scripture together at worship, committee meetings, fellowship events, Bible classes, small groups, or retreats. The practice not only creates space and silence for listening, it communicates a vital message for incarnational churches: The Spirit is in this place, and Scripture is one of the ways the Spirit speaks to us.

There are other ways to encourage listening within our congregations. Rev. Traci Smith is the author of *Faithful Families: Creating Sacred Moments at Home*, and the former senior pastor of Northwood Presbyterian Church (NPC), San Antonio. At the June 2017 meeting of Mission Presbytery, she experienced a workshop called "The Power and Practice of Personal Storytelling" conducted by Mark Yaconelli. It made a lasting impression.

She says,

> Mark taught us by example, asking us to tell our stories to each other with evocative prompts. One was to describe a sacred place from our childhood, and

another was to tell about our first crush. When we were not sharing our stories, our instructions were simple—just listen, fully, with complete attention and no interruptions.

After the sharing subsided, Mark asked some debriefing questions. What was it like to be heard without others interrupting, competing, or making commentaries? For each of us, it was a sense of being accepted and loved. Then he asked us to remember what it felt like in the room as people were describing their crushes. We recalled a sense of laughter and joy, a buzz in the room, clearly showing how listening creates bonds of community.

What affected Smith even more was a question Yaconelli asked her as they shared lunch after the workshop. "You may not be able to host storytelling events," he said, "but how can you bring its power into your daily ministry?"

Smith took the question to heart, letting it guide her and the other leaders of NPC. Here are some changes they instituted.

At least once a month following the sermon in worship, Smith asked people to cluster together in their pews and answer questions related to the message. Every time this happened, someone commented on how meaningful it was to them. The church now encourages Bible studies, committees, and fellowship groups to begin each gathering with a time of sharing based on questions that require a degree of personal disclosure. A good example is the monthly men's breakfast, where a group of guys has learned to open up their lives to each other in deeper, more vulnerable ways. As one participant recently said, "I have known some of these men for decades, but never realized the richness of their histories."

When a married lesbian couple considered joining NPC, Smith knew the church would welcome them, but the question was, "How deeply?" She decided to employ a simple listening exercise as the elders gathered for their monthly meeting. Share a story, she asked, about one person you know who is gay, and specifically tell us—if you know—about how other churches received them. The stories were diverse, and throughout all of them it became obvious that NPC's leaders wanted to extend an unconditional welcome. It was a sacramental moment, illuminating the truth that listening is hospitality made flesh.

When Sarah Clapp and her wife, Elizabeth, joined NPC, they became immediate recipients of this inclusion. This was especially gratifying for Sarah, who grew up in the Southern Baptist tradition and attended a conservative nondenominational Christian school for thirteen years. She looks back on that experience with mixed emotions.

"There are so many negative things I could say. They were hypocritical, judgmental, rich, white, 'know-it-all' Christians. But there were also many positives. That school grounded me in my faith. I received an in-depth, micro-seminary education. They gave me questions without easy answers. They taught me to think for myself and to have my own relationship with our Creator. They showed me how to incorporate spirituality into my daily life. All of this was extremely important during a formative period in my life, ensuring that I had a solid foundation for my faith."

These benefits, however, were ultimately outweighed by the fact that Sarah could never fully be herself. Further, she saw the tragedy of students being expelled for openly declaring their sexual orientation. Later, both she and Elizabeth experienced this exclusivity at other churches, where they were barred from working with children and found closed doors when it came to other positions of meaningful leadership.

In a testimony to the strength of her spirit, Sarah says, "All that judgment and rejection didn't shake my faith, just my faith in people."

Everything changed when they came to NPC.

"Everyone here was willing to listen to the fullness of our stories, and the acceptance has been like coming home. We have had people say to us, 'I wasn't sure about where I stood on marriage equality, but after experiencing it with you and Elizabeth, I have come to embrace it, and now I am sharing the message with my friends.'"

After joining NPC, the Clapps celebrated the baptism of their daughter, Samantha, and Sarah's ordination as a ruling elder. She went on to lead the Membership and Evangelism Team, strategizing ways to welcome *all* people into a community of love and acceptance.

"The longer we were there," says Sarah, "the more we saw how our continual presence worked its way through the hearts of so many people."

Clearly, listening is at the heart of incarnational mission, and as we think about making it a structural part of our congregation's DNA, consider these two case studies.

CASE STUDY: DIVINE REDEEMER PRESBYTERIAN CHURCH, SAN ANTONIO, TEXAS

Founded over one hundred years ago by refugees from the Mexican Revolution, Divine Redeemer (DR) resides in the poorest zip code of San Antonio, Texas. It is a predominantly Hispanic/Latino congregation with about 120 members. Its distinctive, mission-style chapel was designed by

Harvey P. Smith, a San Antonio architect noted for his help in renovating the Governor's Mansion and two San Antonio missions during the Depression.

One of the most remarkable traits of DR is its steadfast commitment to staying and ministering in a challenging neighborhood of a city that consistently ranks as one of the most economically segregated in America. This resolve to stay put has not been easy, requiring deep levels of intentionality.

By the early 1990s, due to internal conflicts, there was a growing separation between DR and the House of Neighborly Service (HNS), a community center with which it has shared facilities since 1929. The church was paralyzed with respect to mission and outreach. During two previous pastoral transitions, the congregation had expressed a desire to reconnect with its neighborhood. And yet, in those same twenty years the relationship with the community had grown increasingly disconnected.

Three seemingly positive changes contributed to this separation. First, the congregation became financially self-sufficient, a good thing for any mission church, but it separated DR from HNS, and both of them from national coordination of their missions. Second, the staff of HNS became community-based, another positive, but not congregationally connected. This severed the only remaining natural conduit of community residents into the life of the congregation. Finally, DR's members, supported by denominational pathways to education, became upwardly mobile. They left the "hood" and purchased homes in more affluent neighborhoods. This exodus left very few members actually living in the *barrio*.

When faced with this kind of membership flight, many churches seek to move to a locale closer to the members.

DR had this option. A sister congregation approached them to consider a merger. They were a white congregation sitting in the middle of an increasingly Latino community and desired a new beachhead for ministry. The two congregations engaged in discussions, but DR decisively discerned that their calling was to remain in their place.

Unfortunately, they were no longer in a real relationship with that very neighborhood.

Rob: I remember asking a question during one of my sermons at that time. "How many of you can name a person who lives in this community?" Only five people were able to do so. That was a turning point. We needed relationships.

A conversation began about hiring additional staff for this effort, and many in the congregation wanted to bring on a Christian educator. The rationale was that this person could reach out with youth programs to kids in the community and assist us with our waning Sunday school program. I wasn't convinced. Our first priority was to get to know our neighbors.

Perhaps the best decision of my tenure was to throw my weight behind the hiring of a position we called a community catalyst. This person was essentially a set of ears whose primary job was to go out and *listen*. Listen to the neighbors who came to the HNS food distribution. Listen to the residents who participated in the senior lunch program. Listen to the church members and their hopes, dreams, and desires for our church. Overall, listen for what we called *spiritual pregnancies*. These were dreams, visions, hopes, and ideas that individuals would articulate for our community, for the church, and for their own lives. The Community Catalyst was to collect these offerings and then begin to connect the dreamers to one another, to weave a web of relationships between members and neighbors based upon our shared hopes and desires.

The result was explosive!

Within a period of three years, we launched nearly a dozen new initiatives to build relationships with neighbors. Critical to this explosion was an additional decision made by the church's leadership board: we would not be afraid to fail. We would give the green light whenever we possibly could, recognizing that some initiatives would survive and others would not.

Here is a sampling of the kinds of ministries DR started during that time, all of them a direct response to the articulated needs in their neighborhood:

- A neighborhood Thanksgiving celebration
- A neighborhood Christmas Posada celebration
- A Bible study with neighborhood women
- A Teen Night hangout evening on the open-air basketball court which later gave birth to an afterschool program for children (PeacePals) and teens (House of Teens)
- An English as a Second Language class
- A Spanish-language Overeaters Anonymous Twelve-Step group
- A reconstituted Boy Scout Troop
- A church and community decompression retreat
- A Back-to-School Blessing
- A Way of the Cross that reflected the sufferings of the community

- A volunteer-led dance-exercise class
- A healing and wholeness contemplative worship service

This surge of new effort was exhausting for DR's leadership, but it was also exhilarating. They were "back in the hood," and all because they had chosen to listen and take risks. Today, some fifteen years later, about a third of the projects launched during that period continue to operate effectively, sustaining relationships between DR and their neighborhood. All of them were born out of making listening a part of their congregation's DNA.

CASE STUDY: MEADOWBROOK UNITED METHODIST CHURCH (MUMC) IN FORT WORTH, TEXAS

The arc of MUMC's history is so familiar it seems apocryphal in America's urban settings. In 1928, two smaller Methodist congregations in Fort Worth's Meadowbrook neighborhood merged to form a new congregation. Like so many urban congregations, MUMC reached a membership zenith, then began a precipitous decline as the neighborhood experienced demographic changes in the 1960s and 1970s. Large groups of African American and Hispanic residents moved into the area. Unfortunately, this caused waves of white flight, cutting into the church's budget and membership.

For many of the members who remained, the result was ultimately positive. Gary Cumbie, a longtime congregational leader and past board chair at MUMC, says, "The folks who have stayed really believe that this is where we need to be."

Several years ago, the church adopted this mission statement: "We are a Christian fellowship embracing our community with hope, acceptance, and unconditional love. We understand that true community change can only occur when we open our doors and hearts to those outside the congregation." It sounds like standard loftiness, yet MUMC lives out this creed by generously sharing its huge physical plant, including the sanctuary, fellowship hall, scores of classrooms, and their Community Life Center (a gym/multiuse facility).

This church is truly an amazing example of opening one's doors! Its facilities are active nearly every day of the week with a breathtaking variety of community groups. Here is a partial list: the local neighborhood association, the East Fort Worth 4-H Club, Girl Scouts, Boy Scouts, Tarrant Actors Regional Theater, karate classes, Early Childhood Matters of Fort Worth, Upward Basketball, Cheerleading, Soccer, a Games Day for older adults, Rotary Club, a Bible study aimed at women who have been homeless and/or victims of abuse. In the summer of 2017, the church hosted Project Transformation, a residency for college students who served elementary schoolchildren in the neighborhood.

All this hospitality requires deep levels of attentiveness. Listening to their members and the streets around them is integral to MUMC's presence. Two ministries in particular highlight this core value.

One is Daughters of Worth, a weekly Bible study and support group moderated by Rev. Denise Blakely, MUMC's associate pastor. It arose from Denise's contact with the many people who come to the church for assistance with food, transportation, and lodging. She noticed that a high percentage of them are women. As she listened attentively to their stories—which included prostitution, drug addiction, and homelessness—God enlarged her heart with a vision.

She says,

What struck me is how the self-images of these
women had been beaten down by life on the streets.
Since our ministry as Christians is to help people
find their worth in God's eyes, to believe that with
God all things are possible, I offered some space to
come together. It's a combination Bible study and
covenant group that has evolved through the Holy
Spirit into a sense of family. It reminds me of the
early small groups of Methodism called "classes,"
chances for folks to gather and support each other in
their spiritual journeys. It has been amazing! These
women celebrate Thanksgiving and Christmas with
each other, and they have begun to reach out to other
women who are alone and suffering on the streets.
They want to mentor them toward a sense of worth
and new life. All of them are learning to transcend
their circumstances and become who God created
them to be.

Another outcome of listening at MUMC traces back
to Lois Bogush, a member in her early eighties. As a girl
growing up in rural Kansas, Lois was deeply affected by the
4-H club her mother established, a woman whose success
with the program earned her a trip to the national head-
quarters in Washington, DC. Lois internalized the 4-H
values of initiative, responsibility, skill mastery, and service.
Later, as a middle school teacher in Fort Worth, Texas, she
founded a 4-H club on campus that touched the lives of
hundreds of students until her retirement.

In her early sixties, while active at MUMC, Lois saw
a wealth of accumulated skill and life experience residing

in the lives of MUMC's members. From an asset-mapping point of view, this was a treasure trove. She petitioned other leaders to consider launching a 4-H club on their campus, a way of reaching out to the community and giving some of this wisdom back to others. The initial reaction was skeptical. 4-H in an urban environment? 4-H in a racially mixed neighborhood of kids whose interests seem decidedly contrary to an old-school program?

Lois persisted, the leadership listened, and today the 4-H club at MUMC, founded in 2000, is thriving. It provides a staggering array of learning projects: from photography to poetry, web design to wildlife study, speed typing to small engine repair, Opera 101 to karate, chess to computer building, public speaking to parliamentary procedure. All this is done in tandem with the community. The club partners with a host of organizations that have shown interest in its target demographic. The Lions Club, Toastmasters, Rotary Club, Optimist Club, and other Fort Worth civic groups contribute funds to sustain the club's program. Businesses including Lockheed Martin, Tandy Leather, John Deere, and JoAnn Fabrics have also joined the effort.

"One vital aspect of this outreach is how it is connecting people across economic fault lines," says Rev. Blakely. "For instance, engineers from Bell Helicopter and Lockheed Martin have given the youth hands-on classes on robotics. In return, these teachers have had a chance to meet inner-city youth and hear their stories. In a world where we often live in parallel universes, the value of this contact is incalculable."

The 4-H club at MUMC has received a number of accolades, and recently hosted a contingent of national and state 4-H leaders. Their purpose was to observe the success of MUMC's club and learn ways to replicate it in other urban environments. To this end, the church's club has written documents that outline their efforts and goals to connect with inner-city neighborhoods.

"Central to everything we do," says Lois, "is the concept of both giving *and* receiving. Our older members, as well as civic leaders, get a chance to share the skills they have developed over a lifetime. It gives them a great sense of being needed and valued. In turn, we expect our youth to give back to the community. It is a requirement for participation in our program, and we offer volunteer opportunities throughout Fort Worth. Every year, we reward the youth who have shown the strongest efforts in serving our community."

Two thriving ministries—a restorative group for struggling women, a 4-H club that expands the horizons of inner-city youth and adults—are just two examples of how listening to people inside and outside the walls of our congregations can lead to life-changing ministries.

DISCUSSION STARTERS

1. Consider again the quote by Paul Tillich that begins this chapter: "The first duty of love is to listen." Describe the meaning of these words from your own perspective.
2. What are some of the obstacles to listening in our personal lives?
3. What are some of the obstacles to listening in our life together as congregations?
4. Look back on some of the examples in this chapter. What are some possible ways your congregation could weave a listening presence into your various ministries and programs?

5. Consider inviting someone whose perspective on your neighborhood or city is different from your congregation's to speak at an event or at a meeting of one of your leadership councils.

PRAYER

Loving God, before we jump into action, help us be still and steep ourselves in your presence. Open our ears and hearts to the lives of our brothers and sisters, especially those whose experience differs from ours. In this way, O God, give us an ever-deepening appreciation for the beautiful diversity of your world.

Chapter 3
TRANSFORMING PARTNERSHIP

> Mission in partnership is a transformational adven-
> ture . . . a risk. . . . There is no way to guarantee what
> will happen along the way to God's future.
>
> —Sherron George

Partnership *always* transforms us, shaping our characters, our spirits, our actions. If we don't experience this ongoing change, we have an acquaintance or sterile contract, not a partnership. We miss the fullness of what God intends for us. Mutual transformation is the hallmark of fruitful collaboration, whether it's in a marriage, a student/teacher relationship, or a corporate merger.

Scripture reveals that this truth is rooted in the partnership between God and humanity, a brazen contradiction of the axiom that God is unchangeable. In his commentary on Genesis 18, Walter Brueggemann takes up the striking conversation between Abraham and God regarding the fate of Sodom. The conventional calculus of the ancient world was that innocent people deserved their fate. The righteous could not rescue them. Yet Abraham urges God to consider an alternative worthy of God's holiness, and his persistent haggling prevails! Brueggemann concludes, "The questions of Abraham carry another possibility which God must now consider. It is the possibility that innocent people have the capacity to save others and the power to overcome the destructiveness of guilt. . . . This is the good news that moves toward Jesus of Nazareth."[1]

We see this same dynamic in the conversation between Jesus and the Canaanite woman (Matt. 15:21–28). At first, Jesus refuses her request to heal her daughter, claiming his ministry is exclusive to Jews. However, like Abraham, she rebuts him, persuading him to change his mind. The faith of this pagan woman amazes him, and he chooses to restore her child.

These stories reveal a God who is willing to be transformed, to experience a compassionate change of heart, all because of a desire to journey in union with humanity. Clearly, partnership is at the core of our faith.

When a church decides to partner with its neighborhood—allowing itself to listen and learn—the relationship has the potential to change both the congregation and the neighborhood. Similarly, when churches partner with other organizations, each of them commits to a makeover, and the creation of healthy partnerships is a tricky business. There are potential pitfalls and problems to acknowledge and address if our relationships are built to survive.

In the church's history of mission partnerships, there are many failures and false starts. We also find notable successes. Although this chapter focuses primarily on our neighborhoods, let's briefly hear some lessons learned by a few individuals who have forged international alliances.

LESSONS FROM ABROAD

In her book *Called as Partners in Christ's Service: The Practice of God's Mission,* Sherron George, former missionary with the Presbyterian Church (U.S.A.), identifies five essential missional attitudes that contribute to healthy partnerships.

- **Respect.** Valuing the otherness of your partner's identity as having equal dignity and worth; expecting there to be differences but staying committed to understanding rather than judgment.
- **Compassion.** The ability to feel the suffering of others, to climb inside their reality long enough to experience it with them, not to fix it, but to *feel* it.
- **Humility.** The ability to recognize the limits of our understanding and perspective, opening ourselves to the unique wisdom that comes from our partner's position in life.
- **Observing and participating.** Learning to balance our *doing* with *being.* Typically, those who initiate local mission efforts perceive themselves as having the answers and capacity to implement predetermined solutions. As noted in the preceding chapter, *listening without doing* is essential to the cultivation of trust and respect. When the time comes for action, it happens with deeper awareness and investment.
- **Receiving and giving.** This is difficult to embody with authenticity. Far too much mission work is a one-way transfer of resources and talent from the haves to the have-nots. This one-sided dynamic destroys real relationships. It objectifies both the giver and the receiver into one-dimensional caricatures that impoverish us all.[2]

Here are a few individuals who have learned to practice these missional attitudes in the contexts of other countries.

Charles and Melissa Johnson began their international mission involvement late in life. It started with multiple voyages to Vietnam in their early fifties, followed by a Peruvian trip with their home church, Northwood Presbyterian,

San Antonio. The next step was short-term volunteer work in the Democratic Republic of Congo. There they sensed God calling them to full-time service. Since 2016, they have been mission coworkers in Zambia through the Presbyterian Church (U.S.A.), partnering with the Church of Central Africa Presbyterian (CCAP), Synod of Zambia.

Early in their travels, the Johnsons experienced a moment of profound compassion. It happened in the Democratic Republic of Congo. They were standing in the breezeway at Good Shepherd Hospital, Tshikaji, when Charles saw a male nurse in scrubs walking toward them. The nurse had something cradled in his arms and was followed by a man and woman. The woman was wailing, and as they came abreast of the Johnsons, the reason was clear. In the nurse's loving grasp, underneath a *kuba* cloth, they saw an infant's arm and leg protruding. The child's parents were following the nurse to the morgue. The Johnsons instantly recalled their own grief at the loss of their son, Holden, several years earlier. Their hearts broke for this family and its loss, and while they never learned the cause of the baby's death, the empathy of that moment transcended all borders.

In their current work in Zambia, the Johnsons have daily reminders of the need to remain humble, respecting the differences of their partners. Charles brings decades of experience in agriculture and business, but despite his considerable knowledge, a large part of his current journey has been listening and learning about Zambian small-farm methods. His primary project is a model farm at Chasefu Theological College, and there Charles relies on the friendship and guidance of Rev. Mapopa Nyirongo. The goal isn't to replace local practices with Western technology but to look for ways, as partners, where Zambian traditions can improve using modern methods.

Melissa works in the health department of the Church of Central Africa Presbyterian. Her coworker, Richard Willima, patiently tutors her in all aspects of Tumbuka culture. At events with Zambian stakeholders in the health arena, he has helped her understand Zambian customs of formality and politeness. Many times, she has found herself wanting to jump right into a meeting and begin discussing the tasks at hand. Mr. Willima has gently reminded her to slow down and follow protocol. In Zambia, greetings and handshakes are mandatory, as are formal introductions (even if you already know each other). Another Zambian practice unfamiliar to Westerners is to pause for several minutes of silence in the midst of a conversation. For an American, this silence can feel awkward and uncomfortable. As she explains, Melissa is learning to wait, to be polite, and to observe the cultural norms:

> As we strive to understand and treasure our differences, we are fortunate to have close Zambian friends and coworkers. They are always open to discussing things which confuse us. They help us grow in patience and humility as we understand at ever-deepening levels that our ways are not always the best. To truly be partners in God's mission, we must have respect for each other and the differences we both bring. We are so blessed to be able to live in this community with those we are serving. We worship, laugh, sing, dance, celebrate, share meals, and mourn with them. We are bound together by our faith as followers of Christ.

Rev. Leslie Vogel knew she wanted to serve in Central America even before she entered seminary. As a senior at Whitworth College, she participated in a semester-long study and service program that visited Costa Rica, Honduras, Guatemala, and Mexico. The closing chapter of the Sandinista revolution in Nicaragua was rocking the region, and Leslie witnessed its political and economic effects, especially the influx of war refugees. That sojourn raised her consciousness and instilled a love for the Central American people.

Leslie's journey has been circuitous, including eighteen years raising children and time serving both Catholic and Lutheran parishes in El Salvador. For five years, she worked as a facilitator for intercultural encounters with the Protestant Center for Pastoral Studies in Central America (CEDEPCA). Her role was to receive, teach, and accompany groups of North Americans who want to experience the reality in Guatemala, a country struggling for justice on many levels.

"Our emphasis," she says, "is to listen and observe rather than jumping immediately to action. This is not always easy with North Americans who gauge their effectiveness through projects of building, painting, and digging. We try to teach that learning from the people is the most important first step. It lays the groundwork for everything that follows."

Leslie has seen the good, the bad, and the ugly when it comes to the development of partnerships. She tells of a group of women engaged in a myopic rush to finish a building project. They instructed a Guatemalan man to saw boards for them, then turned their backs to work in another area. They never paused to learn his history, including his extensive experience as a carpenter in the United States. They were so driven by their notion of "doing good" that they missed the opportunity for a human relationship entirely.

"Basically," says Leslie, "I think the experience impoverished these women rather than enriching them or broadening their horizons. They missed every vital aspect of true partnership. They insisted on being in charge, didn't listen, didn't value this man and his skills. They even walked away without working alongside him. In short, they devalued him, never really encountering him and his unique gifts as a human being. They perpetuated the reality, not just the myth, of the 'ugly American.' "

Leslie can also share positive, heartwarming stories of intercultural understanding. She tells of a fraternal group of men from the U.S. that wanted to assist the Asociación de Padres y Amigos de Personas con Discapacidad (ADISA), a Guatemalan organization that works with families and friends of people with disabilities. ADISA asked them to help clear some land, then lay the foundation for a small dental clinic.

These young men patiently listened to the tutelage of ADISA's master builders, learning how to create iron rebar pillars for each corner. When they got to the phase of constructing the walls, it became clear that their supervisors were expecting to finish the project later, using funds provided by the fraternity. So, rather than push to complete their offering, a compulsion of many Americans, they spent their final day learning about national issues of education, particularly for people with disabilities in Guatemala. They enjoyed a guided tour, shopping and sightseeing as their hosts proudly shared local heritage.

"The experience with these young men left me feeling deeply satisfied," says Leslie. "They learned to receive as well as give, and I know that when they returned to their fraternity brothers in the U.S., they shared a new vision about the adventure of serving—one that includes learning about others as well as themselves. This is the core of partnership."

BRINGING IT HOME

Once again, read the partnership dynamics outlined by Sherron George. Each is profoundly valuable for working with our neighbors wherever we are. Combined, they provide a wake-up call to the importance of maintaining a posture of mutual respect, one that suspends judgment and cultivates a willingness to both receive *and* give. It is a lesson we need to relearn repeatedly.

Rob: One Sunday morning I was scrambling out of my car to begin the relentless series of responsibilities that solo pastoring requires on a Sunday, when I recognized a woman walking toward me. She is a local resident who survives as a sex worker on the street. She regularly asks me for a few dollars, which I sometimes provide, often with an uncomfortable sense that I am likely enabling some habit she has. This exchange is never quick, and I was in a time crunch already, so I tried to make it into the church before she could catch me, only to be nabbed by her exclamation of "Pastor!" just seconds before I safely reached the door. "Hi, Rosie," I replied with a disingenuous smile. "Here," she said. "These are for folks at church this morning," as she handed me a bag from the nearby grocery store. Inside it were a bottle of orange juice and some *pan dulce*. I was taken aback. My first instinct was to say, "That's OK, Rosie, you don't need to do this," knowing that she probably used precious food stamps to buy the items. But a better voice inside me prevailed. I managed to mutter a "Thank you" as I took the bag, giving her a hug and wishing her a blessed day, stunned at my capacity for patronizing judgment.

Everyone has something they can give. Learning how to receive as well as give is essential to preserving the dignity of *all* partners. Rosie was my teacher that morning. She unmasked the superiority and judgment in my attitude and required me to recalibrate my understanding of partnership with my community.

Genuine encounters with others whose life experience is foreign to us can rewrite the pages of our stories. The same is true for a congregation, especially in neighborhoods where the demographics have shifted. These differences can be economic, educational, ethnic, religious, or cultural, separating us into enclaves that have little to do with one another. If we are willing to take risks despite our diversity, tremendous transformation unfolds.

Relationship is *always* the precursor to collaboration. It takes knowing one another to create the trust bridges that foster mutual investment. Once we begin this investment, we start creating a future bigger than ourselves. We move to a new reality beautifully expressed in a poem by Micky ScottBey Jones called "Invitation to Brave Space":

> Together we will create *brave space*
> Because there is no such thing as a "safe space"
> We exist in the real world
> We all carry scars and we have all caused
>   wounds.
> In this space
> We seek to turn down the volume of the outside
>   world,

We amplify voices that fight to be heard
    elsewhere,
We call each other to more truth and love
We have the right to start somewhere and con-
    tinue to grow.
We have the responsibility to examine what we
    think we know.
We will not be perfect.
This space will not be perfect.
It will not always be what we wish it to be
But
It will be *our brave space together,*
and
We will work on it side by side[3]

Creating brave spaces is central to our Christian calling, but too often we church leaders live in silos of our own experience. We become trapped in the constant demands of a congregation's pastoral needs and programs, rarely finding time to build new relationships beyond our boundaries. This can be especially true for inner-city churches where pressing needs are great, and daily phone calls often require urgent responses. A family may need food or help paying an electric bill during the winter. A man is picked up by immigration, and his wife needs assistance navigating the bureaucracy. It can be difficult to prioritize building relationships with others in the face of these emergencies.

But it is not just our busyness that hinders us. On a deeper level, there's a truth operating in many of our churches that may be hard to admit. Too often we have a possessive mind-set that measures the worth of our efforts by the number of people who attend, join, or commit. This sets congregations and denominations against one another instead of in partnership *with* one another and God. The scarcity notion is that there are limited sheep to capture, and we need to do it better than the folks down the street.

> **Rob:** Years ago, during a visit to Central America, I met Pablo Richard, an exiled Roman Catholic theologian then working in Costa Rica. While interviewing him, I asked him about the tension between Catholics and Protestants. His response has guided my philosophy of ministry ever since. He told me, "The scandal of the church is not that we are different, that we see the sacraments differently, interpret the Bible distinctly, or worship and make decisions differently. The scandal of the church is that we attempt to use these differences to work against one another. We seek to *possess* the people of God instead of *serve* the people of God. What we fail to grasp is that the people belong to God and not to us. We should always be using the gifts and uniqueness of our traditions to *serve* them, rather than to *possess* them."

In the spirit of mutual service, every one of our congregations can benefit from transformational partnerships. We may forge them with groups already on our campus, with other nonprofits we have supported in a cursory way, or with sister churches in our city and/or denomination. Whatever our points of contact, the following practices are fundamental to success. You will quickly see how they build on truths from previous chapters.

Practice #1: Listen together, especially to pains and frustrations, then imagine a new future. To state the obvious, if relationships are the fuel for partnership development, then they require time spent listening to each other. *There is no shortcut around this aspect of incarnational mission.* The transformational magic that enables us to meld into partnerships can only arise from long conversations about shared fears, frustrations, and longings for the future.

In his book *Prophetic Imagination*, Walter Brueggemann speaks of the ability to imagine a world beyond the world as it is—a world of partnership, not isolation. Essential to this process is the public voicing of emotions by members of any community. It releases energy and creates the intimacy necessary to envision a new future. Brueggemann compares this to the enslaved community of Abraham's children as they cried out from the pain of slavery, seeking a future of freedom and possibility. Transformational partnerships emerge in a similar way.

Practice #2: Maintain an abundance mentality, recognizing resources that are already present. Rev. Jake Medcalf, pastor of First Presbyterian Church, Hayward, California, describes a powerful truth at the core of his approach to ministry. "Deep in my DNA," he says, "is the idea that God is already at work in any community. We need to join the work that God is already doing." It is essential for all of us to carry this mind-set into possible partnerships, believing we will meet the Spirit there and discover the assets we need to succeed.

Practice #3: Don't let monetary concerns steer the boat! Sadly, many of us in the United States succumb to a capitalist viewpoint that enslaves us into believing that we must identify financial resources before taking any step toward our dreams. Many great ideas are squashed by scarcity-minded church boards whose only response is, "We can't afford to pay for this!"

Brothers and sisters who come from capital-poor environments—here or abroad—often teach us a critical lesson: *we don't need money to start building our dreams.* Begin with the abundant resources at hand. Draw upon the people, experiences, passions, talents, and available facilities. Once you are moving, once you discover your power to make something happen, once you feel the burn of your potential, *then* look for the financial resources to expand that effort. But *never* let money steer the boat.

ABCD teaches that there are two kinds of power: organized money and organized people. Partnerships are fundamentally the latter. It is relationships that create the initial and sustaining power. They provide the trust capital that enables long-term partnerships to succeed. Money will come later as a function of relationships. This is a vital and essential lesson. Most congregations situated in transitional neighborhoods experience a scarcity framework, in part because of being overly focused on finances. Shifting that focus to relational resources is explosive and empowering.

Practice #4: Forge agreements that respect the dignity of each partner, then review them regularly. In Appendix 2, you will find some suggestions for the crafting of space usage agreements. You can easily discover other models with lawyers or your denominational representatives. The point is to forge these agreements with *all* parties involved, respecting each one's dignity and contribution. Rob speaks to the importance of this in the relationship between Divine Redeemer and the House of Neighborly Service, the ninety-year partnership we mentioned in chapter 2.

> **Rob:** We have had notable successes, but it has not been easy. As partners with separate boards, budgets, and staff, we have had to navigate and negotiate

many years together. We've had periods when we were happy and content, as well as times ridden with tension. Until we put a clear partnership agreement in place, we found ourselves fighting too frequently over who is responsible for roof repairs, gas line leaks, or bathroom plumbing emergencies. We were quick to blame each other for not paying a fair share of costs, or for making unilateral decisions.

The time to hammer out a covenant is *not* in the middle of a conflict when trust is low and tempers are high! So, when a relative peace had settled over the realm, we crafted a Covenant Agreement for Cost Sharing. These policies now make it possible for us to quickly address emergencies and crises as they arise. Much more importantly, this deeper definition of our individual roles and responsibilities, including resources we can allocate, shifted us into a more fruitful and stable working relationship.

Happy feelings and a general desire to work together are simply not enough to create a successful partnership over the long haul. Take the time to define and protect the dignity of each partner's contributions and benefits. It is an ongoing process of negotiation, but it is worth the investment.

Practice #5: Take time to play! Rev. Mike Murray is the principal of Creative Interchange Consultants International, a Texas-based organization that consults with businesses and nonprofit organizations intent on shaping healthy relationships. In Appendix 3, you will find six qualities of partnership that he and his consultants have identified. One of the them is taking time to play. It's so important to celebrate at regular rest stops along the timelines of our partnerships. We can do this through holiday events, fairs, open houses, or fundraisers. The key is to find ways for every partner and its constituents to participate in meaningful ways, no matter their ages.

For instance, Divine Redeemer has an annual Neighborhood Thanksgiving Celebration, an evening of worship, song, and feasting. Participants from both their afterschool and senior citizen programs make table decorations. Another nonprofit on their campus contributes volunteers and food from its pantry. The Boy Scout Troop and teen program set up the tables. Church members cook the food and join board members and staff to serve over four hundred people. Neighbors assist in the cleanup afterward. Everyone has a role to play, a gift to give, and a joy to share. This event has come to symbolize the mutually supportive structure that this church and its partners have put in place to guarantee the dignity and respect of everyone with a stake in their shared ministry of hope.

As you forge partnerships in your own locale, here is additional inspiration from two case studies. Both of them provide a natural bridge to the next chapter, "Integrating Our Space."

CASE STUDY: LIVING CHURCH (LC), SAN ANTONIO, TEXAS

LC calls itself "a nondenominational progressive church." It formed thirty-four years ago with a unique purpose— to offer spiritual and material assistance for those dying of AIDS. Initially they served the community by providing logistical and financial support for funerals. Then, as people began living longer, they helped with medicine,

electric bills, and back-to-work clothes for those emerging from months of hospice care. As the community they
served experienced changing needs, the church did its best
to adapt. This partnership transformed them and is still
changing them today.

When the current pastor, Joseph Garrett, arrived in
San Antonio years ago from Fort Lauderdale, he noted a
significant difference in the status of the LGBTQ community. In Fort Lauderdale, LGBTQs had property, political
clout, and influence on the community's direction. In San
Antonio, the combined cultural effects of a large concentra-
tion of Baptist, military, and Roman Catholic populations
were oppressive to the LGBTQ presence.

"People had no power, no voice, and few places to
congregate," says Garrett. "The overall message was to
'stay in the closet.' Because of this, we adapted. Our focus
changed from helping people with basic survival to offering
a gathering space that is affirming and empowering."

In 2016, LC sold its property in an economically
exclusive area of the city to move into a neighborhood of
mixed socioeconomic status. They purchased a large, aban-
doned church campus for half its market value, thanks to
generous equity-sharing by former owners. Believing that
Jesus' example is to give ourselves for others, LC began creating a collaborative community space called Woodlawn
Pointe. It is home to the church, but also has seventeen
"incubator offices" in the rehabilitated school wing of the
property. These spaces host community organizations, arts
groups, small businesses, and an attorney. The diversity
of tenants is amazing: the Pride San Antonio Show Band;
Live Oak Singers; Threshold Singers (who sing hospice
patients to the other side); the American Organization for
Immigrants, which assists refugee women and children

immigrating from Central America; and an interfaith chapel, where a Muslim-styled worshiping community offers
non-Muslims access to Islamic worship practices in order
to build bridges.

Through all of this, LC has maintained a sensitivity
to the resistance many LGBTQ folks have about coming
into churches, places that had too often harbored rejection
and judgment. LC transformed its look and language to
be less "churchy." The former sanctuary, now referred to
as the Auditorium, has been refitted to serve a wide variety of events. There you will find concerts by the tenants,
local political debates, conferences of the LGBTQ Coun-
selor Association, a drag queen pageant, and an Alcoholics
Anonymous celebration during San Antonio's Fiesta called
Fiesta Frenzy. The Fellowship Hall is now the Banquet
Hall and is available for community social events.

"There is something going on here nearly every single day!" says Garrett.

> Our core focus is to provide space to the LGBTQ
> community, but we are not exclusive. So many
> worlds come together here. For instance, while a
> Hispanic family was moving its business into Wood-
> lawn Pointe, their patriarch died. Since they had no
> church affiliation, they approached me to see if we
> could hold a wake. We made the Banquet Hall avail-
> able, and I conducted a prayer service. Jesus' exam-
> ple is to give, to lay down our lives for others. So that
> is what we are doing. We are sharing what we have,
> adapting in *every* way we can.

When asked about the ways he has witnessed transforming
partnership, Garrett says,

At first, each group in our building stayed to themselves and didn't interact. Desiring to change this, I started making a big salad every day at lunch which I brought out to share. We ate together. We shared stories and got to know one another. Once that happened, we began to see ourselves as part of something much bigger. We began to support one another's efforts. For instance, the band sold tickets for a concert by the community choir, the community choir offered to sing in our worship service, and the band and drama groups collaborated on a wonderfully entertaining show for all of San Antonio.

Here is partnership at work. LC has been transformed, reshaped multiple times through its close relationship to the community it serves and its willingness to listen to the needs at hand. But the members of the community have also been transformed into a body that is mutually supportive, recognizing that together they are part of something much grander.

CASE STUDY: CYPRESS CREEK CHRISTIAN CHURCH AND COMMUNITY CENTER, SPRING, TEXAS

When Cypress Creek (CC) was established in April 1972, the congregation decided it didn't want to build a structure that would only be occupied on Sunday mornings. From the outset, they believed that an important way to reveal God's unconditional love would be to use its buildings as outreach tools. So, in 1978 they listened to the community around them, doing a formal needs assessment of residents and organizations. It was a lengthy but richly rewarding process that led to a monumental decision. They decided to partner with twenty-four local nonprofits, all of which provided valuable community services but needed a safe and welcoming place to serve local residents.

After a few years of success with this model, CC and its partners imagined a new addition to their future— a beautiful, state-of-the-art concert facility now known as The Centrum. The Centrum is an 881-seat, world-class performance venue, now well established as Northwest Houston's concert hall. The Houston Symphony Orchestra performs its annual New Year's Eve Concert there, as well as numerous other programs during the year.

Bill Duffy is a longtime member of CC and has served on both the congregation's board as well as the community center's board. He reflects on the church's history:

> These buildings don't belong to us; they belong to God. But we are responsible for them, and we have sought from the very beginning of our life as a congregation to use every facility we build, seven days a week, by sharing them with our community. *Anyone* who can enhance the quality of life for our community is welcomed as a partner! In turn, the community continues to reshape us. The neighborhood is changing, becoming more Latino. The kinds of partnerships that served in the past will need to change to meet the new needs. We can't rest on our laurels.

Sadly, the ravages of Hurricane Harvey in 2017 severely damaged CC's facilities, but because of the myriad partnerships involved, the rebuilding effort has not fallen solely on the congregation. A multitude of partners have responded, offering material and physical support. The

CC campus and The Centrum will rise above the floodwaters to continue their mission of serving all their neighbors.

Today, after thirty-six years of service, those initial 24 partnerships have grown to more than 160 partner organizations serving the humanitarian, cultural, educational, and spiritual needs of the Northwest Houston community. However, the work of listening never ends. CC continues to survey the community it serves, discovering and mobilizing new resources relevant to the ever-changing needs of its community.

Admittedly, the scope of CC's story may seem too far beyond the more humble circumstances of many churches. However, it is a valuable demonstration of the key truths in this chapter. Listen together. Identify assets and allies. Build relationships. Dream together of a new future. Take steps toward that dream. Allow financial resources to flow out of the power of relationships.

This is the core methodology of crafting the lasting partnerships that are transformative for both us and the world around us.

DISCUSSION STARTERS

1. Describe a personal relationship that transformed you in some significant way. How did that relationship occur? What enabled it to be so transformational?
2. How would you describe the current relationship your congregation has with the neighborhood around you? How many neighbors can you personally name?
3. Where do neighbors congregate? Where are the current places (points of contact) that enable your

members to interact with these neighbors? How can you use these places to initiate conversations that allow you to listen to each other's lives and experiences? What can you do to enhance or expand these opportunities?

4. If you don't have any points of contact, with whom in your church can you start a conversation about how to initiate them?

5. Who are some of the people in the life of your church with the time to listen to others in the community?

6. What one step will you take to begin to build a relationship with a neighbor?

PRAYER

Loving God, thank you for partnering with us through the power of the Spirit. Open our hearts and minds to new partnerships with others. Cultivate a deep humility in us that believes we have as much to learn as we have to give. Amen.

Chapter 4
INTEGRATING OUR SPACE

The place God calls you to is the place where your deep
gladness and the world's deep hunger meet.
—Frederick Buechner

Think of a place that has a powerful hold on you. It may be
a family homestead, a setting in nature, or a venue in your
city where you spend quality time. These locations evoke
more than memories; they stir our spirits and connect us
with memories of times past. They help us incarnate in the
real world, however fleeting.

Cultures since the beginning of recorded history
have valued "power spots" or "thin places," locales where
the veil between the temporal and eternal seems to dissolve.
Though we can open the doors of perception to God's
presence anytime, anywhere, we still love to take pilgrim-
ages to these places, reveling in their beauty. It is why Mus-
lims make their Haj to Mecca, Latter-day Saints visit the
Mormon Tabernacle in Salt Lake City, or Sikhs travel great
distances to pray at their Golden Temple in the Punjab.

Our experience of Scripture is also tied to places.
Think of Jacob wrestling with God on the banks of the Jab-
bok, Moses on top of Sinai, Jesus speaking to the Samaritan
woman at Jacob's Well, or Paul and Silas singing hymns
at midnight in a Philippian dungeon. In these and countless other episodes, the settings of the biblical narratives are
integral to the story.

We could learn a lot about the power of place from
indigenous cultures rooted in their homelands. In the great

outback of Australia, Aboriginals practice *dadirri*, a profound way of listening and connecting to the soil of their ancestors. For ancient Hawaiians, a respect for *aina*—the land—found its way into all their religious beliefs. For the Navajos it is the territory between their Four Sacred Peaks, a belonging so powerful that the late journalist Jules Loh said, "The Navajos need no precise survey, no legal deed, no carefully drawn lines of latitude and longitude to know the land is theirs. They know it in their souls."[1]

For many of us, our church is a place that elicits these strong emotions. Sitting in its sanctuary, fellowship hall, or classrooms, we can visualize the faces, relationships, and events that have enriched our lives. As we learn to gratefully map the abundance God has given us, our buildings are a primary blessing. This is true despite the constant care to maintain them, especially with aging facilities.

If our faith stories are tied to our buildings, how can our buildings, in turn, communicate to our communities? In his book *Why Church Buildings Matter*, Tim Cool writes,

"Story" is all around us, in virtually every aspect of our daily experiences, which means that our church and ministry facilities also tell a story. Here are a few important questions to ask about your church facilities:

What stories are your facilities/campus telling?

Are we intentional about the telling our story through our facilities?

Is the story congruent with who we are, who we think we are, what we believe and value, and who we want to reach for Christ?[2]

Intentionality about our church facilities is the focus of this chapter—the urgent importance to maximize their potential not only for current and future members but *right now* for the community in which God has placed us.

Much of the current discussion in redevelopment circles is about repurposing church buildings, especially those that have closed their doors to sacred functions. Some have morphed into cafés, theaters, or centers for nonprofit enterprise. In many cases, this has preserved these historic structures for generations to come. The original sacred purpose is lost, but the architecture remains.

There are also efforts to repurpose space within our active churches. We frame this as the leasing or sharing of rooms that too often lie dormant during the week, their potential squandered. This usage is closer to what we mean by integrating our space, but still misses the mark.

Reflect again on the case studies of Cypress Creek and Living Church in the previous chapter. These are prime examples of integrating our space as opposed to simply repurposing it. What is the difference? *Ensuring that every partner who shares our facility does not drift into a parallel universe.* We refuse to be like ships passing in the night. Instead, we strive to develop shared vision and participation, believing that God brought us together for a unique purpose. We are certain there is abundance waiting to emerge.

Too often, we rush to share our buildings without attention to these long-term redevelopment goals. Examples of this are common: preschools that employ massive amounts of square footage, but whose students and families have no real connection to the host church; nonprofits that incubate on our premises without ever hatching hybrid projects in partnership with us; and Boy Scout Troops, Twelve Step meetings, yoga and Zumba classes, or other outside groups that have no cross-fertilization with our congregation or its mission.

Let's put it bluntly. Integrated space means that we *only* share our facility with those who truly want to partner, contributing to the increased spiritual energy and redevelopment of our congregations. This is not selfish or self-serving. It is a simple recognition that if our sacred places are to remain as beacons of faith for generations to come, we *must* position them for the long term.

What do we mean by "increasing spiritual energy" as a component of incarnational mission? Sometimes our alliances with those who share our buildings lead to increased income, membership, or attendance. What a blessing when this happens! Often, though, the benefits are less quantifiable. Increased spiritual vitality is one such value. We can spark this vigor by interpreting the mission of these other entities back to our church membership, linking our lives with theirs. As we connect the dots, we discover the Spirit of God at work in our midst.

For instance, one congregation hosts a number of flourishing Twelve Step groups. Only a few participants from these fellowships have ever crossed into church membership. Still, the leadership has found a moving way to highlight this behind-the-scenes partnership. Several times a year, individuals in recovery give heartfelt testimonies during worship, reminding the congregation that the simple act of providing space is impacting lives. This knowledge increases the church's spiritual energy, its sense of itself and its mission.

In another congregation, the preschool was disconnected from the church membership. After strategy sessions with the school board, the church's music director formed a choir of the preschool children. Once a quarter, these children sing during worship services, highlighting the partnership. The preschool also assigned a member of its staff to write stories for the church's monthly newsletter, increasing awareness of its impact on families.

In these examples and others, the first step toward integrated space is a frank appraisal of how we view our space. Is it congruent with our purpose and vision? Does it communicate that purpose and vision to our community? Addressing the issue of our church structures is complicated, especially if our buildings are aging and beset with deferred maintenance issues. It will require a difficult decision between two opposing views of church property. Shall we make decisions based on *an antiquated sense of ownership* or upon *a resurrected sense of stewardship?* The choice we make as a community will ultimately define our identity and our future.

AN ANTIQUATED SENSE OF OWNERSHIP

Every brick, beam, shingle, stained-glass window, and pew of our buildings came into being through the generous, often sacrificial giving of faithful members. Many of them were pioneers in our communities. They participated in the campaigns for these structures with a vision of prosperous ministry for the future. If still alive, they have spent countless hours in the classrooms, fellowship halls, and sanctuaries of these places that are sacred to them. The church is their second home, familiar down to the details of how they have arranged the library or parlor furniture. They have faithfully paid the bills for utilities, repairs, and insurance. In short, the brick and mortar have survived due to their dedication.

We've all heard the phrase "familiarity breeds contempt." When it comes to our church facilities, it is more apt to say "familiarity breeds an antiquated sense of ownership." It is far too easy for longtime members to forget an essential theological premise that informs incarnational mission. *Ultimately, the church building belongs to God.* Not to the entity whose name is on the deed. Not to a mortgage company. Not to the judicatory body. Not to the members themselves, no matter how hard they have worked to erect and maintain it.

This structure belongs to our Creator, and we as stewards *must* maximize the use of every square foot in advancing the kingdom of God.

Once again, this requires communal conversion, because second only to the gifts of our members, our physical buildings are the greatest assets at our disposal. The critical question to answer is, "How can we integrate our buildings not only to serve God's purposes now, but as a way of positioning our church for generations to come?"

Raising this question, as many leaders will testify, often results in powerful resistance. Change is hard! This is why we need champions of a different paradigm.

Krin: I met a champion like this during my time as pastor of First Presbyterian (FPC), Pomona, California, a city in east Los Angeles County. Once a quaint Victorian hamlet surrounded by orange groves, Pomona became engulfed by L.A.'s urban sprawl, a change that included drug trafficking and violence. The church sat on a volatile fault line between two warring gangs rooted in the Mexican Mafia. Most of FPC's white members fled to the suburbs, reducing the rolls from thirteen hundred to under two hundred.

On February 1, 1985, faulty electrical lines ignited the church's beautiful structures built in 1907. Though the education wing escaped by a benign (some said miraculous) shift in the wind, the entire sanctuary burned, its Tiffany-designed dome exploding in a small mushroom cloud seen for miles in Los Angeles County.

As I studied FPC's recent history prior to an interview, I learned that a debate had raged within the leadership of the congregation. Should they flee Pomona and relocate to a suburb, or should they rebuild on their original site? Eventually, the faction intent on remaining in Pomona won the argument. However, when they built their modern new sanctuary, they turned it away from the streets, large metal gates guarding an interior courtyard.

Shortly after I became pastor, I encouraged bolder leaders to open the church to the neighborhood. We began partnering with a number of nonprofits, as well as the Intervarsity Christian Fellowship (ICF) at the local Claremont Colleges. On the top floor of our educational wing were hallways filled with dusty rooms that had long been inactive. We offered them as apartments to students with ICF connections. We charged no rent or utilities, simply asking that these students help energize our ministry with the youth of inner-city Pomona.

Slowly, blessedly, the church began to resurrect with new activity. Voices rang out from the hallways and gymnasium. A second-floor computer lab had daily usage. In the midst of this, I remember a meeting when a particular elder voiced a concern. "As chairperson of the Buildings and Grounds Committee," he said, "I warn us to think about what's happening to our facility. All this traffic is wearing out the carpet, both in the hallway and . . ."

"John, let me interrupt," said another elder, a man whose family stretched back to the founding of the church. "I appreciate your protection of our assets, but I have a different perspective. For years, so many of us have prayed for the sound of young voices in this congregation. Now they are here, and though they may be of a different class or color than our old guard, it should fill us with gratitude. This church had become like a mausoleum, and now we are seeing signs of resurrection. I can only say 'Praise God!' and I hope the rest of you will join me."

A RESURRECTED SENSE OF STEWARDSHIP

As we begin to experience the abundance of gifts present in our congregations and neighborhoods, as we learn to listen before acting, as we forge new partnerships, a miracle unfolds. We experience what Paul said in Romans 8:11: "If the Spirit of him who raised Jesus from the dead dwells in you, he who raised Christ from the dead will give life . . . through his Spirit that dwells in you."

This is the power of the resurrected Christ in our midst, the promise of abundant life, and it applies to a new sense of stewardship about our buildings. Rather than focusing on the burden of their upkeep, we focus on our renewed belief that God has fresh purposes we are only beginning to glimpse.

For many years, an Episcopal lay leader named Andrew Weeks traveled around the country presenting a seminar titled "The Magnetic Church." Gifted with humor, he used phrases that participants remembered for years afterward. He told them to avoid the "vampire trap," an outlook summed up by "we need new blood in this church." That mentality, he said, is concerned primarily with what the church needs, not the world around it. "Are you trying to fill empty lives or fill empty pews?" he asked. "If you fill empty lives, you will have full pews."

One of Weeks's teaching methods always caused a stir. As soon as people got seated in the conference room, he would tell them, "Get up! That's right! Put down your gear and follow me." He would then lead them outside the church and across the street. Once the class was assembled, he would say something like this. "Look across at this place you call your church home. You see it through the lens of familiarity, which can become a form of blindness. I want you to reach up and symbolically take off that set of lenses, whether they are rose-tinted or gray. Put them in your pocket. Now, replace them with a set of new lenses and imagine you are seeing everything as a visitor for the first time."

What followed was a tour de force meant to change the participants' mind-sets. Weeks would start with outside signage. Is it fresh and readable, or evidence of deferred maintenance? Does it clearly give the times for classes and worship? If it has a rotating message, does that message appeal to the general population, or just Christians? Moving inside, he would solicit a similar inventory. Are there clear signs telling the locations of bathrooms, classrooms, and child care? Does the building in general communicate a sense of airiness, light, and hospitality, or does it seem like a slightly grungy throwback to distant decades? As he passed particular rooms, especially those that seemed musty or deserted, he would say, "Hmmm, when does this space get used? More importantly, does it ever *really* get used? Who in this community needs to find a place right here?"

By the time this guided tour was over, many people were speechless. Quite literally, it was the first time they had seen their church facility through the eyes of visitors from the community. It is this fresh awareness, this new perspective, that can lead to a resurrected sense of stewardship, a belief that every single aspect of our buildings is meant to be employed in service through a fully integrated approach. Churches intent on this style of stewardship will build the following practices into their congregational culture.

New Directions with Current Partners

If you are already sharing your building with other groups—preschools, A.A. meetings, nonprofits—the first order of business is to reevaluate the quality of these relationships. Are there meaningful connection points? Is there some kind of cross-fertilization? If not, how can we take steps toward a common sense of mission? As we mentioned in the previous chapter on transforming partnership, spending time in dialogue and relationship building is key to this new direction. There may be many hours of listening necessary to set the groundwork. Start now with this investment of time, believing it will lead to abundance.

New Expectations for Future Partners

If you are considering new partnerships under your roof, make sure that your expectations are clear from the beginning. This is far more than negotiating a joint-use agreement. It means establishing guidelines for mutual investment in each other, a way of communicating our belief that we are *always* better together. Guard against the false notion that just because our buildings have more activity, we are going to experience resurrection. Far too many churches have found that even with multiple groups under their roofs, they have not seen increased spiritual energy. Always remember that the goal is integration, not just space sharing.

A New Understanding of Place

This means putting on the lenses that Andrew Weeks proposed in his workshops. Every leader and every area of ministry must ask themselves some basic questions: How can we make this place that we love so dearly a powerhouse for mission? How can we consider deployment of our space as part of our future plans?

As you consider the possibilities for your congregation, here are some case studies. The first one uncovers a need for *all* congregations given the cultural realities that surround us. The other two show churches that have clearly made the shift to a resurrected sense of stewardship.

ART IN SACRED PLACES

Partners for Sacred Places (PSP) is a dynamic, creative nonprofit founded in 1989. They describe themselves as "the only national, non-sectarian, nonprofit organization focused on building the capacity of congregations of historic sacred places to better serve their communities as anchor institutions, nurturing transformation, and shaping vibrant, creative communities."[3]

One of their innovative projects is Art in Sacred Places (AiSP). Its original premise was prompted by a simple observation. In many cities—especially those with skyrocketing rent prices—artists, theater troupes, and dance and performing groups are priced out of the market. They have no place to call their own for rehearsals and performances. PSP asked a question that drove their research in three cities: Baltimore, Austin, and Detroit. How could the underutilized space in many sacred places be linked to these artists for a fruitful collaboration benefitting the community at large?

Karen DiLossi, director of AiSP, articulates the vision of the project, especially its intent to integrate, not just repurpose:

> Artists and sacred places often have a lot more in common than they realize. My passion stems from bridging the gap and helping them align their missions and visions, drawing lines to show how they can be mutually beneficial. Seeing them make these links is satisfying and rewarding, particularly when it leads to stronger, healthier, and more open communities. It shouldn't just be a marriage of convenience because of location or amenities, but one of common purpose in which one another's mission is expressed via the partner.

Austin fit the research criteria perfectly. One of America's fastest-growing cities, it is a mecca for the arts, known as the "Live Music Capital of the World," but also filled with burgeoning dance, theater, and filmmaking scenes. Its world-renowned South by Southwest Festival, primarily focused on music, has expanded to include these other flourishing areas of the arts. However, given the city's explosive growth, lease prices are exorbitant, beyond reach for artistic groups in their early stages of development. How could underutilized space in congregations and temples fill the gap?

Lynn Osgood is the executive director of GO collaborative, a nonprofit partner of PSP in Austin. She coordinates AiSP matches between artists and sacred places. As the process has unfolded, she uncovered a cultural phenomenon that may be widespread for American congregations trying to link themselves with their neighborhoods.

"We have found that many churches are open to space sharing with artists," she says, "They may need to develop new muscles for turning outward, but there is genuine excitement about the possibilities. It is the arts community that is reticent. The Austin arts scene is social-justice oriented, and many within the community feel a distrust toward religious institutions. We are trying to overcome this hesitancy by highlighting the wonderful chance for synergy."

Osgood's findings are revealing. Clearly, churches that have been working tirelessly for peace and justice need to communicate their efforts. We need to share our identities more clearly. This telling of our stories is central to our community connections. If we are going to attract additional partners, we cannot be hidden in plain sight. Whole generations may not fully understand how progressive churches have evolved to incarnate God's purposes in our world. We can tell our stories through our new partnerships, through social media, and through our engagement in public events. Unless people hear about the nature of our ministries as well our compelling vision for the future, how can we expect them to be drawn to our campuses?

FIRST CHRISTIAN CHURCH, FORT WORTH, TEXAS

First Christian Church of Fort Worth (FCC), born in 1855, is the oldest continuously operating church in its city. The town's first doctor, Carrol Peak, and his wife, Florence, helped establish the congregation, which initially met in the Peak home. The church's first pastor was A. M. Dean, an itinerant farm worker who carried a hymnal and a pistol. Later pastors included famous Texan Mansell Matthews. Joseph Clark and his sons Addison and Randolph, founders of the college that became Texas Christian University, also preached at the church.

Members laid the cornerstone for the current building on March 21, 1915, completing construction in 1916. An example of Renaissance Revival, the beautiful structure immediately became an iconic part of Fort Worth's urban landscape. It has been on the National Register of Historic Sites since 1983 and received the Fort Worth Historical and Cultural Landmarks Designation in 2006.

Beginning in the 1960s, after a storied century of service to its community, FCC began to experience major membership decline. As the church entered the twenty-first century, membership was at less than 10 percent of its historic peak. The upkeep and use of their massive building became increasingly problematic, especially since they rarely used large portions of it. The congregation considered moving, but the majority of members stubbornly refused to budge.

During 2006 and 2007, FCC participated in New Dollars / New Partners, a program offered by Partners for Sacred Places (PSP). The program uses asset-based community development principles to reorient congregations to their potential for a glorious future. This exposure to new ideas and methods germinated into Glimpses of Reign in 2011, a congregational program whereby the church welcomed new ventures into its building: exercise classes, cooking seminars, and community outreach organizations. However, the effort was not fully integrated. These new groups existed in parallel realities and did not adequately help the congregation address long-term problems of maintenance, sustainability, and the spiritual energy of the congregation.

True partnerships evolve and transform the participants. The strong relationship between FCC and PSP had set the foundation for what happened next.

The University of Houston College of Optometry and the University of Incarnate Word in San Antonio were looking to expand eye care services in Fort Worth, specifically aimed at the homeless and disadvantaged. PSP helped broker a deal between these colleges, the City of Fort Worth, and FCC. The church was a perfect match. Its central location was accessible to those in the most desperate need of care, and the church had the physical capacity to house both the clinical needs of patients and the instructional needs of optometry students. A vision arose for a long-term partnership.

Change is always difficult, especially when a church has so many memories invested in its building. FCC also had a long history of dysfunction and division within its congregation. To most members, it seemed that there could be no serious discussion about change of *any* kind without toxic polarization. Predictably, the initial response to opening their doors for an eye clinic provoked stiff resistance. How would such a massive integration affect them?

Rev. Tom Plumbley, pastor of FCC says, "Church self-understanding is *so* critical. Like many congregations in our situation, we used to be something way more than we are now. We were proposing a change to our church's culture, and this change required a new mind-set. It also required great patience and understanding."

Plumbley and the church leaders who attended the PSP sessions were the driving force behind this shift in the church's perspective. They formed a committee to evaluate the proposal, intentionally including those who felt most threatened. They made sure that everyone was heard, painstakingly intent on reaching the broadest possible consensus.

The result was a communal conversion, with a turning point in July 2012. "The membership came to a new realization," says Plumbley. "We are tied to this building, but we aren't just the past. We are the future, too, and we had to change the idea of our building being a museum." The congregation awakened to a new vision, realizing how this partnership opportunity allowed them to expand their mission *and* preserve the facilities as a landmark for future generations.

The Community Eye Clinic of Fort Worth, which occupies the entire second floor of FCC, opened in 2013. It is now the largest clinic of its kind in America, shining as a model of integrated reuse for congregations in communities everywhere. Plumbley looks back with gratitude for what has happened.

"Since the 1950s," says Plumbley, "members had stubbornly resisted one offer after another from investors who wanted to redevelop this valuable piece of property in a booming city. The only problem was that after a while, they had lost their reason for resisting. This watershed decision to partner with the Eye Clinic changed everything. It has given the church a new self-image, new self-esteem, and new vigor for its mission. For instance, we recently became a part of Room in the Inn, a national program that opens churches to the homeless. This kind of forward-thinking outreach would never have been possible prior to the Eye Clinic."

What a great example of how maximizing the use of our facilities leads to increased spiritual energy and living hope for the future.

CASE STUDY: BAPTIST TEMPLE, SAN ANTONIO, TEXAS

"You could hear a pin drop from one end of the building to the other," says Rev. Jorge Zayasbazan, pastor of Baptist Temple (BT), describing the church when he arrived in 2009. "The facility was primarily used on Wednesday nights and Sunday mornings, and the offices simply shut down on Fridays."

To understand the weight of this description, you need to envision the magnitude of its setting. Baptist Temple (BT) is a sprawling, multifloor complex of eighty thousand square feet, including a gymnasium. Though the church had a history of helping its neighbors stretching back to the Great Depression, the scope of its mission had obviously dwindled.

At the same time, the church's neighborhood needed its influence more than ever. The Pew Research Institute consistently ranks San Antonio as one of the most economically segregated cities in America, with many impoverished neighborhoods that are especially hard on children. BT exists in what is called the Eastside Promise Zone. It is at the intersections of historic Anglo, Hispanic, and African American neighborhoods that have all seen economic decline. In his 2014 State of the Union Address, President

Obama designated this area as one of the first five Promise Zones, a national initiative to revitalize high-poverty
communities. The aim is to ensure that everyone, regard-
less of their zip code, has equal access to opportunity and
prosperity.

Jorge relished the chance to reengage BT as a part of
this vision. A native of Havana, Cuba, raised in Miami, he
got his education on the streets, in the Marines, and at New
Orleans Baptist Theological Seminary. He describes himself as an "entrepreneurial church leader experienced in
developing new ministries and planting new churches." He
has sponsored, hosted, and/or coached dozens of start-up
fellowships, including Haitian, Korean, Hispanic, Filipino,
and deaf congregations.

He was just the kind of leader Baptist Temple needed.
Though he welcomes the traditional pastoral duties of
preaching, counseling, and administering the sacraments,
he says this about his calling: "My primary job as pastor
here is to open up our space so that other groups can further their influence on our city."

This resurrected sense of stewardship regarding its
building has vaulted BT into a rapidly expanding era of
ministry. On any given day, the building hums with activity
from a host of organizations that have found a home in this
place. We list them here in order to highlight the stunning
depth and breadth of their outside-the-box inclusion:

- Five smaller, multilingual congregations that meet
  in the building, including a church for the deaf, that
  combine their youth and children for Sunday and
  Youth Group activities, creating higher energy, a
  sense of Spirit, and a sharing of leaders

- A thrift store and food pantry
- A community garden
- Abundant Life Ministry, teaching skills like money management, parenting, healthy living, as well as spiritual formation and leadership development
- Christian Women's Job Corps
- Good News San Antonio, a summer program that offers hands-on urban experiences for youth and adults; groups from numerous denominations come to participate
- Basketball leagues in the gym
- Girl Scouts
- Bible study fellowship
- A Wednesday night community meal for anyone experiencing hunger
- Immanuel Motorcycle Ministry, whose focus (besides their Harley-Davidsons!) is ministering to convicts, paroled felons, and families whose loved ones are still incarcerated
- An Early Childhood Learning Center with over one hundred students
- The Highland Park Gifted and Talented Academy, an open enrollment, tuition-free charter school that follows Stephen Covey's *Seven Habits of Highly Effective People* through the "Leader in Me" program
- Housing for students of the Baptist University of the Americas, who receive free room and board with the agreement that they will participate in BT's neighborhood outreach

Zayasbazan and the other leaders of BT see themselves as permission givers rather than agents of control.

They admit that it is *always* a challenge to integrate so many programs, given our natural human tendency to go our own ways. But when the synergy is firing on all cylinders, the results are amazing.

BT's vacation Bible school in the summer of 2017 is a prime example. All of the resident congregations helped with the planning and implementation, as well as the Early Childhood Learning Center, the charter school, and a local ministry to African refugees. Two hundred children attended, helped by ninety leaders of all ages, in what Zayasbazan describes as a "spectacularly international event."

A few weeks later, BT hosted a Back to School Fair that included backpack distribution, health exhibits, food, music, and vouchers for their thrift store. Eight hundred people converged on their campus, overwhelming their best-laid plans. Zayasbazan laughs when describing it, saying, "We learned a lot about dealing with crowds that day!"

This church has come such a long way in both utilizing and integrating its buildings. You may have been able to hear a pin drop ten years ago, but now it would be virtually impossible given the joyful voices that echo through its hallways. And this congregation never stops evolving. Even now, they are writing grant proposals to help them address the deeper issues in their neighborhood, with a lofty goal of breaking the cycle of poverty.

Zayasbazan has a lot to say about churches and their relationship to their facilities.

"The spiritual wealth of a congregation extends to the spiritual power of their building. Think of it in terms of the parable of the Talents. We don't want to be like the servant who hid his talent and never invested it fully in ministry. We don't want to simply be protectors of our facilities, worried about wear and tear, content with preserving them and never maximizing their potential. To use the parable analogy, I have seen churches that the Master took away because the people were afraid to engage and reinvest."

You won't find this fear or lack of vision at BT. In a recent grant application, Zayasbazan wrote this description of the congregation: "We are a family of churches and nonprofits bringing God's love to southeast San Antonio in creative and practical ways, adapting to both the shifting needs of the community and the changing skill sets of our many partnerships."

What a powerful description of integrating our space!

DISCUSSION STARTERS

1. Share a memory about a place that is especially dear to you. What gives it this resonance in your life?
2. Share a memory about your involvement at your church, no matter how long you have been there. Can you see how this place has been a sacred setting for you?
3. If you look at your congregation and its leadership, are you more invested in an antiquated sense of ownership or a resurrected sense of stewardship?
4. Do you currently share your facility with outside groups? If so, have you found a way to partner with them, or are you like ships passing in the night?
5. Think of a space in your facility that is sorely underutilized. Brainstorm with your group about possible ways it could be integrated for Christ's mission.

PRAYER

Loving God, your love extends to all times and places. We thank you for the gift of our church's facilities. Help us, as good stewards, to invest what you have given us in ways that advance Christ's purposes in our community. Amen.

Chapter 5
SUSTAINING THE VISION

Come, Lord, stir us up and call us back. Kindle and
seize us. Be our fire and our sweetness. Let us love. Let
us run.

—Augustine of Hippo

Initiating change is arduous. We who catalyze it will often
be at the center of anxiety that stirs our congregations.
Rabbi Edwin Friedman talks about how important it is
for leaders to remain calm in the midst of this turbulence.
In his book *A Failure of Nerve: Leadership in the Age of
the Quick Fix*, Friedman defines this kind of leader as one
"who has clarity about his or her own life goals . . . [and
is] less likely to become lost in the anxious emotional pro-
cesses swirling about."[1]

Given the price many church leaders pay to navigate
their congregations into new futures, it would be a shame
to see these hard-won changes dissolve. How can we help
ensure that new paradigms and practices remain present for
the long term? How can we develop a clarity that moderates
the anxiety of everyone involved?

Long-range planning and stewardship emphases are
certainly a part of this. You can find numerous books and
specialists to help you accomplish these ends. For purposes of our discussion, we will focus on two vital aspects
of sustaining a vision: *Spirit-filled worship* and *mentoring
new leaders*.

SPIRIT-FILLED WORSHIP

Some things remain constant. Imagine standing on the balcony of a high-rise building, gazing out over a teeming metropolis that boasts millions of residents. You see freeways clogged with traffic. Jets land and take off from a nearby airport. The sounds of a bustling city surround you like white noise, intense and industrial.

Now, imagine that someone cuts off the water supply for this urban landscape. It will begin to dry up in a matter of days. Without trucked-in emergency supplies, it will morph into ghostly ruins, wind whistling through its concrete canyons like a postapocalyptic nightmare.

Shift analogies. Think of the millions of advertisements that air every day across this planet. They scream at us to purchase the latest gadgets in our technological world. Computers, tablets, game consoles, smartphones, home security systems, all of them relying on planned obsolescence to mine our consumer dollars. Now, imagine stripping away the electrical grid that feeds them all. Batteries will die, screens will go dark, the world will slowly descend into medieval candlelight.

Just as our world needs the basics of water and electricity, the local church needs vibrant, life-giving worship. A congregation will always be, first and foremost, a worshiping community. Worship of the living God is what distinguishes us from nonprofit charities, no matter how many of them we count among our partners. Worship is the warp drive, the furnace, the nuclear reactor that fuels our mission.

But what if our worship is unengaging, even arid? Many people, when asked why they did not return after visiting a church, will say, "I didn't feel stirred by the worship." The same answer echoes from members who slip out the back doors, never to be seen again. Can we take a real and sober look at ourselves? Can we remove our glasses of familiarity and see our worship through the eyes of visitors, the unchurched, or members who are comfortably numb?

Church leaders will often blame our culture for a lack of Sunday attendance, claiming that other activities—especially sports—crowd out the cultural priority for worship. Rev. Marcia Mount Shoop, pastor of Grace Covenant Presbyterian Church, Asheville, North Carolina, challenges us with a different perspective. "It's easy to blame society's obsession with sports for encroaching on our Sundays," she says. "But churches need to look in the mirror. Why are sports more enticing than church? Is it because sports are exciting, while church is boring to many people?"[2]

Boring . . . how can we *ever* let that word describe a worship service, a sermon, a piece of music? Far too often, worship becomes like painting a picture by numbers. We dutifully assemble the liturgical pieces, making sure they are the right color, but the final product seems hollow and two-dimensional. Robert Schnase, in the worship section of *Five Practices of Fruitful Congregations*, says, "Without passion, worship becomes dry, routine . . . and predictable, keeping the form while lacking the spirit."[3]

We would change that lowercase spirit to Spirit, challenging us to lead worship in a more Spirit-filled way. Mainline Protestants, wary of emotionalism, can unwittingly resist the Spirit's movement. Yet, we also believe that the Holy Spirit resides in each of us as a guide and comforter. It is the light within that longs to be ignited.

The term "Spirit-filled" does not assume a certain style of worship. It is not an implied criticism of any particular wellspring of liturgy. We use timeworn terms like traditional vs. contemporary, high church vs. low church, liturgical vs. evangelical, but these dichotomies lead to crippling states of mind. They cause us to focus on the form of worship rather than its function. *That function is to lead people into the presence of the living God.* It is not the style that matters, but the Spirited energy with which it is imbued.

People need this infusion of God's presence, because so many of us have become numb to the Divine in our midst. So much of the sacred is stripped from our lives. Our consumer culture lulls us into deeper ennui, substituting materialism for the presence of God. Years ago, Tony Campolo warned of this trend in his book *Wake Up, America! Answering God's Radical Call While Living in the Real World.* He gives numerous examples of consumer goods sold with a promise of spiritual fulfillment. He cites an older commercial that showed a throng of people gathered on top of a hill. They represented all races and cultures on our planet, joining hands in a unity this world has never known. Was it a symbol of the kingdom of heaven? Was it a call for racial reconciliation? No, it was a commercial for Coca-Cola!

By linking eternal spiritual qualities to temporal products, our culture systematically obscures the presence of Spirit. Campolo put it this way:

> In our TV ads, it is as though the ecstasy of spirit experienced by a Saint Teresa or a St. Francis can be reduced to the gratification coming from a particular car, and the kind of love that Christ compared to His love for His church can be expressed by buying the right kind of wristwatch 'for that special person in your life.' In all of this media hype, things are sold to us using the promise that our deepest emotional and psychological needs will be met by having the right consumer goods.[4]

Every Sunday, like refugees from a secular wasteland, members and visitors at our churches come to worship with a yearning for something more. In various degrees of self-consciousness, they are aware of an organic longing to connect with the very Source of Life.

This is why worship truly matters, and why worship leadership is a saving art. Our words, our prayers, our music, the flow of our liturgy—all of it has eternal significance in countering the secular conditioning that surrounds us like water around fish. In worship, we reveal the oft-forgotten truth that we are spiritual beings living a physical life on this planet.

No matter what worship style we adopt, underlying principles help bring us into the presence of the living God, best practices that fuel worship that is more incarnational. We call them *remembering our purpose, understanding our context*, and *becoming multilingual.*

REMEMBERING OUR PURPOSE

It bears repeating until it is a mantra for worship leaders. Every aspect of our services—every song, prayer, and sacrament—has the singular purpose of leading people into the presence of the living God. We lose this fresh perspective when we focus on the form rather than the function.

Krin: I'll never forget a Worship Committee meeting at a church I served. One of its members was new to the congregation, a quiet woman in her early thirties who was rapidly getting involved in our ministry.

Like too many churches, we were in the midst of conflict over blending styles of worship. Not

everyone—no surprise—was excited by the changes
we had introduced. The conversation went on and
on, perseverating over issues of form, not function.
The young woman listened attentively, and when
there was a gap, she asked if she could share.

"I had a dream a few nights ago," she said. "I saw
our congregation on Sunday. You were at the pulpit, Pastor, and there were many people in the pews.
However, when I looked more closely at all of us,
it was like one of Magritte's surreal paintings. Our
upper torsos and chests were replaced by bird cages,
and in each of those cages was a white dove pecking
at its steel enclosure.

"You looked down at your manuscript, Pastor,
then out at the congregation. You put down your
pages, stepped out of the pulpit, and walked to the
floor, quietly looking out at all of us. You reached
down to the clasp that confined the white dove in
your ribcage and released it, setting the bird free.

"Suddenly, all of us began to do the same thing,
opening our cages and setting our doves free. They
rose from the pews and gathered above us in the
sanctuary. The last thing I remember was that the
flock formed into an image of a single dove hovering
over us, its wings stirring the air."

She paused with a beguiling smile. "That's all,"
she said.

We were quiet for a moment, a rarity for that
contentious committee, trying to absorb what was
clearly a message from God. I immediately thought
of Jesus speaking to the Samaritan woman at the
well in the fourth chapter of John. She asked him
about the proper place to worship. Was it in the

mountains of Samaria, as her ancestors prescribed, or was it at the Temple in Jerusalem that was the center of the Jewish spiritual universe? Jesus responded, "Woman, believe me. A time is coming when you will worship the Father neither on this mountain nor in Jerusalem. . . . A time is coming and has now come when true worshipers will worship the Father in the Spirit and in truth. . . . God is spirit, and God's worshipers must worship in the Spirit and in truth." Looking back on that committee meeting, I know it did not solve any problems immediately. But I do know that I personally reexamined my worship leadership on Sundays, moving from a manuscript to an outline. I left more room for spontaneity. I learned to trust in the Spirit as an act of surrender.

UNDERSTANDING OUR CONTEXT

This entire book calls us to incarnate precisely where we find ourselves. For some, this means the multicultural streets of an inner city; for others, the manicured lawns and orderly avenues of a settled suburb; for others, a country landscape where neighbors live miles apart; small towns, mid-size cities, metropolitan centers, each with unique characteristics. Robert Schnase says, "Passionate worship is contextual, an expression of the unique culture of a congregation. Communities have their own distinct patterns, voice, and language for loving God authentically."[5]

It has *always* been this way. From the beginning of Christian witness, the capacity to effectively communicate the gospel was grounded in the life experience of those who were receiving and giving Christ's light to the world. After

the Second Vatican Council in the mid-1960s, Roman
Catholics began to call this *enculturation*: the situating of
the gospel within a particular cultural experience.

The synthesis between culture and faith is not only
a cultural demand, but also a faith requirement. . . .
Faith will not be fully possessed nor faithfully lived
unless it becomes part of the culture.[6]

Rev. Barbara Holmes, in her book *Joy Unspeakable:
Contemplative Practices of the Black Church*, speaks of
enculturation within her context:

All things draw from the same wellspring of spiritual
energy. This means that the sermonic and religious
can be mediated through a saxophone just as effectively as through a pastor. . . . The need to create
impermeable boundaries between the sacred and the
secular is . . . a much more recent appropriation of
Western values. . . . Historically, most efforts to wall
off the doctrinal rightness and wrongness of particular practices failed. Instead, hearers of the gospel
enculturated and improvised on the main themes so
as to tune the message for their own hearing. Given
Christianity's preferential option for the poor, the
cross-pollination of jazz, blues, and tap with church
music and practices could be considered the epitome
of missional outreach and spiritual creativity.[7]

Father Jose Marins was a theological advisor for the
Latin American bishops at the Second Vatican Council. He
says that authentic presentation of the good news of Jesus
always involves five things:

- Message: Jesus Christ
- Messengers: Those who bring the message
- Means: The methodologies they employ
- Media: The media utilized within these methodologies
- Milieu: The social, political, and religious context within which the message is communicated[8]

Only *one* of these doesn't change, the message, because the message is a person, Jesus Christ. To communicate Jesus' teachings to a unique people in a unique time of history, all the others *must* change.

It may seem obvious, but the significance and history of this is too often lost. Just think of the first efforts to share the gospel. The messengers were only twelve men, chosen because they were eyewitnesses to Jesus and his ministry. They walked, two by two, into their immediate locale to "bear witness," since only the testimony of two men could reliably do so, according to Jewish law. They spoke only to Jews. They had nothing written or recorded, no visual aids to assist in their proclamation. They used only their own language, memory, and Jewish Scripture.

Now, imagine if the Christian community had never allowed these limited aspects of witness to change. Fortunately, that is not what happened! Very quickly in the book of Acts, we notice how *everything* began to evolve. New messengers emerged who were not among the twelve. Men *and* women began to share their experience not of a direct eyewitness account of Jesus but of his teachings passed on to them. The message spread into new contexts of the larger Greco-Roman world. The conflict over circumcision forced more *deculturation* from Judaism in order for the gospel to *enculturate* among Gentiles. The experience of Jesus was then written down. Letters, not just personal face-to-face witness, were employed. Ships traveled with the message to regions far beyond Palestine. Though the good news remained constant, all other elements *had to change* to enable authenticity.

For the first three hundred years, Christian worship occurred within homes to avoid persecution and detection. Once Christianity became legitimized, the shift to basilicas radically changed the nature of these gatherings. The very architecture of a *basilica*—with a raised platform (where the magistrate sat) and a lower area for the common people—created expectations of a separate leadership. Who was going to sit in the chair? This led to the rise of a clergy class, something that was not part of the communal gathering of homes. The experience of worship as "the people's work," which thrived during the home-church era, began to fade as clergy took a central role.

Today, we see similar dynamics as congregations struggle with traditions of music, liturgy, architecture, seating arrangements, pulpit and table positioning, leadership expectations, and preaching. So much of what passes for worship in our churches is simply a repetition of what we have inherited. There is little effort to consider how we should *enculturate* within the new reality of our time. The exodus of the Millennial generation from our communities is tied to this. They are searching for something more authentic, a church that is not chained to mimetic repetitions that feel disconnected from their lives.

"Worship wars" are often fought around the misperception that certain practices are "not our way," when in fact *our way* over the course of history has been—though often begrudgingly—to engage in *constant* change. The church has spent centuries debating worship style and content, often arguing about the wrong questions. What's more biblical? Is this "correct"? What if, instead, we asked questions like these:

What is organic to our community? How does the DNA of our community inform our worship habits? How is worship an authentic expression of *this* community's love for God?

The problem for many churches is that we hold so tightly to our practices and invest so heavily in our preferences that we cannot consider what is actually *essential* about our worship. How is our worship relevant in a post-Christian environment, both inside and outside our doors? Is our goal self-perpetuation? Or is it to bring glory to God in this time and place?

For some churches, the desire to attract new members leads them to import a style or format that has no relationship to the church's DNA. Chasing trends and the hot new thing, we end up failing outright or giving birth to a completely separate, nonorganic expression of our community.

Beth Watson, worship and arts director for Shepherd of the Hills Presbyterian Church in Austin, Texas, has thought deeply about these issues. Her congregation is creatively crafting a style of worship that both honors its history and stretches it into something new. She describes the essence of enculturated worship in this way:

> Authentic worship for us at Shepherd of the Hills means that we have diverse music delivered with excellence. We look for expertise and talents within our community, and then seek ways to incorporate them in worship. We resist debates over preference, and instead seek to engage a dynamic, open approach to our worship experience, eager for the Holy Spirit to blow and lead us. We worry less about "what is right" or "appropriate," and more about how we can create experiences that give God glory, and worship that opens us to ongoing transformation.

What follows are a few examples of new and engaging ways to think about worship. One of them, Farm Church, is a result of an initiative called 1001 New Worshiping Communities, launched by the Presbyterian Church (U.S.A.) in 2012. Its purpose is to begin 1,001 new worshiping communities using new and varied forms of church for our diverse and changing culture. Its basic premise is to think outside the box.

Farm Church is a congregation in Durham, North Carolina, that literally meets—and works—on a farm. It expresses its purpose this way: "Farm Church's mission is to gather a Christ-centered community around elements of soil and food, to break bread together, and to leverage all the resources of a farm to address food insecurity in our community." Durham County is about 20 percent food insecure, with close to fifty thousand women, men, and children living at or below the poverty line. At its core, Farm Church works to address this reality. Sunday mornings find the congregants not only singing and sharing but with their hands in the soil—planting, weeding, turning compost, and harvesting.

"We often say that we blur the lines between worship and work at Farm Church," says Ben Johnston-Krase, Farm Church's pastor. "Our liturgy truly is 'the work of the people,' *limos ergos*, who come to plant, harvest, and share locally and organically grown food with neighbors. We are not a church that has a few garden projects; rather, gardening is at the heart of how we practice being church together."

Farm Church is still new, and as it grows and deepens its roots, it is forming more relationships with neighbors, such as those who frequent the food pantry outlet for their fruits and vegetables. This engagement, coupled with the desire to grow in understanding poverty, has led Farm Church to shape elements of worship that are mindful of the larger systems of racism and inequality that lead to food insecurity. Recent services have included experts speaking on these issues and letter-writing campaigns urging local and national politicians to work harder on behalf of those who are oppressed and marginalized in our communities.

Dinner Church, birthed by St. Lydia's Lutheran (ELCA) in Brooklyn, New York, is an enculturated worship experience crafted out of an ancient rite found in the *Didache* but designed to respond to the context of urban young adults. Dinner Church meets in a storefront used during the week as a collaborative work space. On Sunday and Monday evenings, volunteers transform it into a sacred space for intimate, participatory worship that includes chants and a vegetarian meal that integrates the Eucharistic elements of broken bread and a shared cup. There is a Gospel reading followed by a communal sharing of personal stories that resonate with the words offered by a "preacher" who may or may not be ordained clergy.

The experience responds directly to a number of distinct realities in the lives of urban young adults: isolation; late-weekend job schedules as artists, musicians, and food servers; vegetarian food preferences; and a desire for participation and dialogue rather than didactic, top-down teaching.

Rev. Bob Wollenburg is the interim pastor at St. Lydia's. In his seventies, Bob says, "The style of worship at Dinner Church was initially hard for me. My training was traditional, and the level of intimacy and intellectual curiosity of the participants here at Dinner Church was quite challenging at first! Over time, however, I have come to love and appreciate the investment and participation of these young people, and the meaningful relationships that this form of worship makes possible."

The evening ends with a time of personal prayer for one another, a circle of call-and-response singing, and a closing benediction. "Then," Bob says, "everyone pitches in to wash and dry dishes, clear chairs and tables, put away tablecloths. It truly is a community effort!"

For a number of years, Rev. Carrie Graham, pastor of the **Church Lab** in Austin, Texas, has created dialogue space in her living room for people of widely different religious traditions, many of them Millennials. The experience has changed her.

"What worship means to me has been radically transformed by my work with the Church Lab," she says. "I now believe that at the core of worship is our surrender to the Holy Spirit's guidance, informed by what I have seen unfold in agenda-free human engagement."

These are just a few of the sacred moments that have occurred in the sanctuary of her home:

- Witnessing a Jewish member of the LGBTQ community and a Latter-day Saint activist, who actively works against policies for gay marriage, choose to spend time together, mutually doing all they can do to appreciate one another.
- Watching a transgender Jewish atheist recently returned from serving in the Israeli army sit down with a devout Muslim friend to discuss the Israel-Palestine conflict.
- Hearing a board member of the pro-choice National Association for the Repeal of Abortion Laws describe how every time he gets irritated with "the other side" at political rallies, he imagines that they bear the face of his pro-life evangelical friend from his Church Lab group. "I picture her face because I love her, and if I

can love her, I can envision the possibility of loving my other political opponents as well."

"Moments like these provoke me to wonder," says Graham, "to feel my heart widen and surrender as though my hands were raised in the air and I was belting out my favorite worship song. It's a natural, involuntary gratitude to God for getting a glimpse of the kingdom in a space shared by unlikely friends."

Consequently, when Graham plans worship for the pastor collaboratives she facilitates, she intentionally includes voices from outside their homogenous experience—songs from Kesha, slam poetry from the African American experience, movie clips critical of the church, and others. Her hope is that as we begin to listen to those other voices, we just might experience some of the same worshipful wonder that comes from learning from people who are different from us.

"The moment of surrendering a situation to the Holy Spirit, even in the most practical of ways, resonates deeply with me," she says. "It is an invitation to witness God do something unexpected, something I didn't realize was possible or have the imagination to conceive. It is to be in awe of that experience, and then to respond to its challenge through the transforming power of God's love. It is the freedom to be recklessly generous as the Spirit moves among us.

"Thanks be to God!"

MENTORING NEW LEADERS

A common visual technique in movies is the establishing shot, panning over a landscape or city to set the scene. Vast deserts and great pyramids take us to Egypt. The Eiffel Tower or Arc de Triomphe begin the narrative in Paris. Views of Central Park, the National Mall, or the Golden Gate Bridge immediately place us, respectively, in New York, Washington, or San Francisco.

From there we move to the action, the story at hand, the microcosm of our concern.

Apply this analogy to the sweep of church history and its two thousand years of dedication to the gospel of Jesus Christ. We see its rise through the Roman Empire, its spread around the globe, its intolerance as well as inclusivity, its wrangling over theology that led to countless schisms. If we move from this establishing shot, zooming in from billions of faithful, closer and closer, we come to the fundamental level of our movement: the individual disciple. In one form or another, each of them has answered this baptism and confirmation question from the *Book of Common Worship*: "Will you be Christ's faithful disciple, obeying his word and showing his love?"[9]

Now, start with the establishing shot of your congregation. Move to a particular group of disciples in your midst—those who are phasing into positions of leadership, perhaps for the first time. They represent one of the most valuable assets of your church. Their influence can be enormous in sustaining your vision for years to come.

However, we will never fully discover and employ their gifts without taking on the task of mentorship, the painstaking and compassionate shepherding of these members into new roles. This is not just about passing on creeds or articles of faith. Classes that give a working knowledge of Christian and denominational history, as well as local polity, are obviously important. Sharing our church's unique traditions is also necessary, because every leader must first incarnate within a congregation's culture before implementing change. *However, we do not want conformists as future leaders.* We want visionaries, creatively tuned in to their own gifts and the corporate gifts of our churches. We want listeners eager for partnership, emboldened by the Holy Spirit.

Mentorship is not easy. It is an untidy, time-consuming process. Jesus said we would be "fishers of people," and fishing is a messy business. Perhaps because of this, many otherwise forward-looking congregations have neglected this key component of leadership development, a mistake that can have long-lasting ripple effects.

Rob: Mentoring is one of our weakest areas at Divine Redeemer. As a smaller congregation, we struggle to fill our leadership slots every year with willing candidates. It is not uncommon for new members to be quickly targeted as potential elders, lured into service by promises that "it isn't much work." They soon discover that there is plenty to do and few who are willing to help them learn the ropes. Like babies who graduate from an infant float class, they are dropped from the diving board into the deep end of church leadership. We rarely put in the amount of personal time and energy to help them feel like they're not drowning!

I have experienced a lot of failure in this regard, and I consider it one of the most urgent growth areas for my own pastoral development and our congregation's health. Further, I know I am not alone in this realization! Early in my ministry, a mentor gave me a powerful image. Every church leader should have one hand held by someone who is discipling them into maturity, and the other joined to a newer leader whom they are also mentoring. The image is compelling—a chain of disciples receiving wisdom and passing it along, a self-sustaining, vital linkage that ensures the development of future leaders. The hard truth is that few of us manage to prioritize this essential discipline. Instead, we are fragmented in our attempts to support, encourage, and build up emerging leaders for our church communities.

In his book *The Joy of Discipling*, E. Stanley Ott describes the mentorship process as "withness": God with us, and each of us with each other. He reviews the many times in Scripture when God said, "Do not fear, for I will be *with* you." Moses, Joshua, David, and many others received this assurance. One of the historic names for Jesus is Emmanuel, which means "God with us." On the final night of his ministry, Jesus promised the Holy Spirit to his disciples, saying in John 14, "If you love me, you will keep my commandments. And I will ask the Father, and he will give you another Advocate, to be with you forever."

Being with others in a mentorship capacity is how leadership is "caught," not just taught. It is a two-way relationship, one where both the teacher and student believe they have life lessons to share with each other. It is a partnership marked by intimacy and vulnerability. Ott comments on this in describing the experience of a friend.

On one occasion Bob shared how he was counseling a man who was facing the toughest crisis of his life. Bob said, in effect, "I do not know the answer to your problem, my friend, but what I do have is a heart to place alongside your heart." This is what it means to be . . . "with"—the sense of sharing life at its deepest levels. We place our hearts alongside each other.

Discipleship is friend with friend, heart with heart,
loving Jesus Christ and loving one another.[10]

Anyone who has been in a position of church leadership knows how challenging it can be. It tests our minds,
hearts, and spirits. It can strain our very faith. It means
understanding our own spiritual gifts and how we can
work synergistically with others. It requires love, patience,
and self-reflection. But it can also bring us moments of
great joy as we discover the Spirit using us to advance the
causes of Christ.

How do we share both the challenges and pleasures
of this journey? A church that is intentional about mentoring new leaders will build into its culture a number of
important realities.

An Eye for Emerging Leaders

Think of the church as concentric rings of involvement. On
the periphery are those who visit, followed by those who
stay, then those who get involved in an aspect of ministry,
and finally an inner circle of leaders. This nucleus should
never be arrogant, exclusive, or nepotistic. The fundamental tools of our calling are the basin and towel, reminding us
of Jesus washing his disciples' feet. We humbly recall Jesus'
response to those very disciples when they asked him how
to excel: "The one who would be great among you must be
your servant" (Matt. 23:11).

In a church intent on mentoring, the inner circle of
leaders will always keep its eyes focused outward, including on first-time visitors. They will have a mind-set of abundance, believing that God will bring to their congregation the
exact individuals needed to carry on a vision for the future.

A Mandate to Include and Invite

This mandate means that existing leaders in a congregation have woven a basic practice into their lives. They intentionally include and invite others, especially potential new leaders, into a relationship with them. They submit themselves to the task of mentoring. This requires time, and if we set low expectations with our existing leaders, they may never carve out a place in their calendars to intimately mentor others.

Busyness can undermine incarnational mission. Our heads filled with practical details of ministry, too often we miss the living substance of our faith—both the presence of the Spirit and the precious individuals God has given us as partners. Mentoring means slowing down and embracing both God and others.

A High Value on Personal Transparency

Remember, this is not about wielding authority; it is about humility and service. When we share both our successes and failures with another human being, it opens the portals to sacramental moments. We invite others to walk alongside us in the messy journey of our lives, and most often they will reciprocate. In these moments, we are truly on the road to Emmaus with each other.

Mutual vulnerability is a gift. In his landmark book *The Wounded Healer*, the late Henri Nouwen spoke of the power we release when we open our lives to one another. He summed this up beautifully in a devotional based on his writings,

> Nobody escapes being wounded. We all are wounded people, whether physically, emotionally, mentally, or spiritually. The main question is not "How can

we hide our wounds?" so we don't have to be embarrassed, but "How can we put our woundedness in the service of others?" When our wounds cease to be a source of shame, and become a source of healing, we have become wounded healers.[11]

Churches could learn so much from the recovery movement, especially its model of each person having a sponsor.

Krin: My sponsor and I were different in many ways. Our concepts of God, or a Higher Power, were radically different. Our politics were diametrically opposed. Our life experiences had taken us on vastly different journeys. But we shared one thing in common: a disease that had brought us to our knees and threatened to take our lives. We were like the traveling group of lepers who Jesus met at the border of Samaria, both Jews and Samaritans banding together because of their common condition.

My sponsor was direct with me—sometimes hard, sometimes gentle—but always inviting me to learn the timeless truths of the Twelve Steps that have saved the lives of millions of people.

I will never forget doing Steps Four through Seven. This is a process of doing a "searching and fearless moral inventory" of ourselves that stretches back as far as we can remember. It is not an exercise in self-flagellation but a new recognition of the character traits that have led us to mistreat others and ourselves. It is meant to show us the ways that fear, resentment, and pride have enslaved us.

Step Five requires a confession of this inventory to God and another human being. Though I had always valued openness in my life, the prospect of baring my soul so completely caused anxiety. Would I feel ashamed? Would my sponsor, even subtly, judge me for my character flaws and actions?

When I was finished, I felt drained, but also relieved at subterranean levels I hadn't imagined possible. My soul sighed. I looked at my sponsor as a broad smile spread across his face.

"Welcome to the human race," he said. To me, that comment sums up the mutual submission and compassion that are at the core of mentorship.

CASE STORY: COVENANT PRESBYTERIAN CHURCH, AUSTIN, TEXAS

"If we are truly embodying the gospel—the transforming, dynamic power of God in our lives—then others will be attracted to it," says Rev. Thomas Daniels, senior pastor at Covenant Presbyterian Church (CPC) in Austin, Texas. "I *expect* the church to grow if this is true, but we don't *try* to grow the church. Our objective is to intentionally develop people who live and reflect the mercy, justice, and love of God. We believe that if this happens, more people will want to be part of it."

CPC has intentionally organized itself around this conviction. As new leaders are sought, the most important qualities the church looks for in people are those who already embody its core values: "to encourage one another to follow Jesus wherever we live, work, and play," and its essential practices of solitude, service, and community. It is the incarnation of these attributes that drives leadership selection, not length of membership, age, or experience.

Once in a leadership role—whether as staff or lay leader—every person is asked to identify personal growth areas they want to work on in their lives, articulating them in measurable terms. Together with a supervisor/mentor, these goals are set by every leader for a nine-month period (September through May) with established time frames for defining goals (September); reviewing/reflecting on progress, challenges, successes (January); and evaluation at the end of the season (May). Summer is a time to integrate the learnings and begin formulating growth areas for the next year. In addition to individuals, committees also set goals within this same framework. This is an intentional church-wide effort to personally embody the gospel, coupled with a clear and ubiquitous system of accountability to others. It is an intentional process of reflection, a powerful praxis.

In many ways, CPC is engaged in a full-scale effort that resembles core aspects of the recovery movement's sponsorship process. Every leader is required to have a mentor/supervisor who regularly assists them in defining goals, then holds them accountable to these goals. This is how new leaders are forged.

"The fruit we have seen," says Daniels, "is that our leadership has a commonly articulated sense of direction. We are defining 'success' in the same way, seeking to journey together toward common goals. I believe this gives us greater purpose and greater results both individually and as a congregation."

DISCUSSION STARTERS

1. Recall an especially meaningful time of worship you experienced. How would you describe it to another person?

2. Rev. Carrie Graham says, "I now believe that at the core of worship is our surrender to the Holy Spirit's guidance." What does this mean to you?
3. How can worship at your church be more open to the movement of the Holy Spirit?
4. E. Stanley Ott describes the mentoring process as "withness." On your own spiritual journey, has there been someone who came alongside you as both a companion and guide? Share this memory with someone.
5. Look at the leadership development process in your congregation. How intentional is it? Does it include the process of mentoring? If not, what changes can your leadership team make to insure this happens for the future?

PRAYER

Spirit of the living God, tune our hearts and minds to your presence living in each of us. Give us courage to surrender to you, as well as the compassion to journey with others who will carry on Jesus' ministry for generations to come. Amen.

CONCLUSION

Very truly, I tell you, unless a grain of wheat falls into the
earth and dies, it remains just a single grain; but if it dies,
it bears much fruit.

—Jesus of Nazareth

The evidence is everywhere: shrinking rolls, declining
budgets, empty classrooms, missing generations, so much
gray hair in the pews that people joke by saying, "There's
a lot of snow on the roof!" It has been a half century since
demographers began alerting us to the decline in mainline
Protestantism. We don't need statisticians to point out the
obvious. We all know churches that shuttered their doors
and sold their property, their witness to their communities
consigned to the annals of history.

We are also regaled regularly with solutions about
"how to save the church." Every few years, there is a new
method for renewal and transformation, some of them
very inspiring. Meanwhile, our denominational execu-
tives design downsized forms of government to account for
dwindling mission dollars. We tighten our belts again and
again until it seems there are no notches left.

In light of this reality, we are not offering easy
answers. Our overarching message is that mission comes
first, and that if we incarnate the way God has called us, the
future of the church will be what it will be. God will have
God's way.

However, we have also seen how incarnational mission fans the flames of a church's vitality, giving it a new

sense of purpose. We have seen the power released when a congregation mobilizes *all* of its abundant resources—its history, its people, its facility. This conversion leads to a pouring out of our lives, a worshipful response to the One who has given us everything.

It is helpful to remember Paul's famous words in Philippians 2, most likely a first-century hymn: "Let the same mind be in you that was in Christ Jesus, who, though he was in the form of God, did not regard equality with God as something to be exploited, but emptied himself, taking the form of a slave, being born in human likeness" (2:5–7).

Here is the eternal pattern of the Incarnation. Jesus did not use his advantage or privilege as a trump card of power. He did not stay separate from the world around him. He listened with compassion and became available to people, adapting to their realities and teaching in parables they could understand in their vernacular. He emptied himself as an act of service that has guided us for centuries.

Is this our calling? Self-emptying rather than self-preservation? We believe so, but we also know it is scary for leaders who see their roles as maintaining the ABCs we mentioned in the Introduction: **a**ttendance, **b**uildings, and **c**ash.

Remember that the most frequent commandment in Scripture is, "Do not be afraid." The church of Jesus Christ has lived, worked, and died in eras equally as challenging as ours. All the doomsaying about perishing in a "post-Christian culture" only diverts us from our mission.

J. Herbert Nelson, stated clerk of the Presbyterian Church (U.S.A.), challenged his denomination with these strong words.

·

Rethinking ministry is difficult. Implementing new
ideas and establishing them is even more difficult. . . .
Simply put, the world is not the same. The needs of
people have changed. . . . Generational cultures are
far different than in my years of growing up. Ministry
and community needs are continuously in flux. I use
the words "transformative change," because change
without transformation could simply be understood
as rearranging the deck chairs on the *Titanic*. Transformative change requires a significant spiritual investment. It also requires a divestment of self-interest.[1]

We bicker over that word "divestment" when it
comes to withholding our support from corporations
engaged in unjust practices. But if we apply the term within
the context of this book, divestment means emptying our
limited negativity and receiving God's abundance, letting
go of our judgment of our neighbors and celebrating their
gifts, silencing our self-preoccupations to truly listen, dying
to our insistence on having our own way and reaching out
to grasp the hands of new partners, taking off the lenses
of familiarity and seeing our surroundings (including our
buildings) through the eyes of a waiting world, surrendering to the Spirit's movement rather than our own clever-
ness in worship, and clearing our busy calendars to pass the
torch of faith to others through mentorship.

Jesus had it right: "Those who want to save their life
will lose it, and those who lose their life for my sake will find
it" (Matt. 16:25).

We leave you with an expression used by commu-
nity organizers and civic leaders: *anchor institutions*. These
enterprises, like universities and hospitals, are rooted in their

local communities by mission, invested capital, or relationships to customers, employees, and vendors. Because of their influence, they have the potential to bring crucial and measurable benefits to citizens of all ages.

There is growing consensus that churches are unsung anchor institutions. A landmark study titled "The Economic Halo Effect of Historic Sacred Places" examined ninety Protestant, Roman Catholic, Eastern Orthodox, and Jewish congregations in Philadelphia, Chicago, and Fort Worth. It focused on numerous ways that our churches bring economic and social value to our communities.[2]

The results were astounding, showing that, on average, sacred places provide a value to their communities that far exceeds previous notions. One of the major underlying themes of the study is that this value is often unappreciated and uncelebrated not only by the community but the very members of these churches.

Your congregation is an anchor institution for your community! When all is said and done, the lifeblood of Christ's movement will *always* be the local church. It is the staging platform for mission, the beachhead where we help bring the kingdom of God to earth. And despite all its challenges, we hope you believe wholeheartedly in its future.

Let us review the best practices in this book one final time.

Communal conversion. When our churches are coming alive, we turn away from scarcity to abundance, away from ourselves and toward our neighbors. We see that God is already at work within us and around us. We realize that the abundance we need is already present, and that our neighbors have lessons to teach us that we never imagined.

The DNA of listening. Listening to God and to others is the foundation of incarnational mission. Only by taking the time to hear each other's stories—beginning in our pews, then fanning out to the community around us—will we clear the way for God to do something new and exciting.

Transforming partnership. Every partnership should be a nexus of transformation in our lives. Through listening and humility, we discover that we have as much to receive as to give. Partnership requires deep attention to relationship building, but the time we spend will pay temporal and eternal dividends.

Integrating our space. We can share our space, but it is far more powerful to integrate it. This means that every partner under our roof understands and embraces a vision of mutual investment in each other's purposes. We are better together, and the more we integrate our common mission, the more we experience spiritual synergy.

Sustaining the vision. There are many aspects to keeping a vision alive in a congregation. We call for mindfulness in two areas that are tried and true:

1. Surrender to a fresh infusion of the Holy Spirit during worship, seeking new ways to connect with God's presence beyond timeworn categories of traditional vs. contemporary. We must strive for authentic expressions of worship that honor the context and people with whom we live and serve;
2. Build into our DNA a process for mentoring new leaders. The intentionality with which we do this will help us ensure the mission of Christ for coming generations.

We consider it an act of partnership to share this book with you. And we pray that you will continue to be encouraged in your meaningful work wherever God has placed you. We recall the words Paul spoke to the church at Philippi, a group of believers surrounded by a Greco-Roman culture that was often hostile toward them. We share Paul's words in closing.

"I thank my God every time I remember you, constantly praying with joy in every one of my prayers for all of you, because of your sharing in the gospel from the first day until now. I am confident of this, that the one who began a good work among you will bring it to completion by the day of Jesus Christ" (Phil. 1:3–6).

God bless you in your place!

SAMPLE ASSET-MAPPING WORKSHOP

Thinking Inside the Box

Let's take a candid look at our traditional ways of thinking and how they affect us.

What Is Asset Mapping?

Asset mapping helps us recognize the strengths and gifts we have as a congregation and how to leverage them for growth and outreach.

Identify Physical Assets of the Church

Write down at least three assets of your church. These include buildings, equipment, objects.

Identify Individual Assets or Gifts You Personally Can Give to Your Community

- Things I know something about and would enjoy sharing with others: art, history, books
- Things or skills I know how to do and could share with others: carpentry, sports, cooking

Source: Courtesy of The Growing Field

- Things I care deeply about: environment, social justice, children, civic life

Identify Associations

Write down at least three associations you are a part of or that exist in your community. These are voluntary groups, networks, and organizations.

Identify Institutions in Your Community

Write down at least three institutions in your community. These are public agencies, schools, nonprofits, private businesses, parks, etc.

Post It!

Post all of your assets on a blank wall. Do not organize or categorize these.

Putting the Pieces Together

As you look at the wall of assets, both your own and others, begin to brainstorm how two or more could be connected to accomplish something. Name that action. Is it a project, event, demonstration, or something else?

Sharing and Voting

Each group will share the action plan they came up with. After listening to each group's idea, go stand by the one you would be involved with and support.

Appendix 2
SUGGESTIONS FOR JOINT USE AGREEMENTS

- Have the outside group sign a "facilities use agreement" that (1) provides the group with a mere license to use the property, (2) contains a hold harmless and indemnification clause, and (3) states that the church provides no supervision or control over the property when being used by the group. An attorney should prepare this document.
- Have the church named as an additional insured under the group's liability policy.
- Review the group's liability policy to ensure that it provides adequate coverage and does not exclude sexual misconduct.
- If the group's activities will involve minors, have a written acknowledgment from the group that all workers have been adequately screened.
- Check with the church insurer to determine coverage issues in the event the church is sued as a result of an accident or injury occurring during the group's use of the church.

Appendix 3

SIX DIMENSIONS
OF A PARTNERSHIP

1. A Clear Definition of the Target

Unless you both agree on the objective you are seeking to accomplish there is little hope of achieving it! If each partner considers a different set of criteria important to evaluate success, then you may never both feel successful!

2. A Clear Definition and Recognition of Each Partner's Contributions

This is essential if partners are to engage one another on equal footing with mutual respect. If all the resources are coming from one side and all the benefits accrue to one partner, there is little hope for long-term partnership. Someone is going to feel taken advantage of, or disrespected as 'less-than' compared to the other. Either of these conditions will kill a relationship . . . sooner or later.

3. A Defined Process for Negotiating Interdependencies

How we can expect to lean on one another in times of vulnerability? Can we count on one another's resources in a time of need? Can one partner lend an extra hand when

Source: Courtesy of Creative Interchange Consultants International

126

required if the other is handicapped? How willing are we to accommodate each other's extraordinary needs for space, for example? Careful, though, because if one partner is *always* doing the leaning and *never* doing the supporting, the other partner will quickly feel burdened or abused.

4. The Ability to Manage Crisis and Change

Change destabilizes, period. That must be acknowledged and not ignored. The management of crises must be jointly done without blaming or hiding from one another.

5. The Ability to Manage Conflict

Conflict should be handled in ways that *increase* partnership. When conflict is mishandled it breeds mistrust. If conflict is handled transparently, giving equal attention to *both* the relationships at stake and the issue that needs to be resolved, then trust is cultivated and the partnership is strengthened.

6. Taking Time to Play

Enjoy the successes, celebrate the accomplishments, and find ways to enjoy each other beyond the working relationships. "Eat, drink, and be merry!" counsels the preacher in Ecclesiastes.

Appendix 4

BIBLIOGRAPHY OF
ASSET-MAPPING RESOURCES

The following list of resources is not meant to be exhaustive, but suggestive of the literature that is available for those desiring to pursue asset-based community development. Others have created more extensive collections of resources, some of which are cited here:

BOOKS AND ARTICLES

Cunningham, G., & Mathie, A. (2002). *Asset-based community development—An overview*. Paper presented at the Asset-Based Community Development Workshop, Bangkok. http://www.synergos.org/knowledge /02/abcdoverview.htm .

Diers, J. (2004). *Neighbor power: Building community the Seattle way*. Seattle: University of Washington Press.

Green, M., Moore, H., & O'Brien, J. (2006). *ABCD in action: When people care enough to act*. Toronto: Inclusion Press. Introduction available from http:// www.mike-green.org/pub/abcd_book_introduction .pdf.

Kretzmann, J. P. (2010). Asset-based strategies for building resilient communities. In J. W. Reich, A. Zautra, &

J. S. Hall (Eds.), *Handbook of adult resilience*. New York: Guilford Press.

Kretzmann, J. P., & McKnight, J. L. (1993). *Building communities from the inside out: A path toward finding and mobilizing a community's assets*. Evanston, Ill.: Center for Urban Affairs and Policy Research, Northwestern University. Introduction available from https://resources.depaul.edu/abcd-institute/publications/Documents/GreenBookIntro.pdf.

McKnight, J. (2013). *A basic guide to ABCD community organizing*. Evanston, Ill.: Asset-Based Community Development Institute. Available from https://resources.depaul.edu/abcd-institute/publications/publications-by-topic/Documents/A%20Basic%20Guide%20to%20ABCD%20Community%20Organizing(3).pdf.

Snow, Luther K. (2004). *The power of asset mapping*. The Alban Institute. This resource offers a step-by-step process for engaging in asset mapping in a variety of contexts with a congregation.

ADDITIONAL RESOURCES

Building Your Community—How to Get Started: An Asset-Based Community Development Tool Kit. The tool kit draws on the theoretical basis developed by John Kretzmann and John McKnight from the Asset-Based Community Development Institute at Northwestern University (now housed at DePaul University). This kit adapts the ideas of ABCD to a local Australian environment and is designed to encourage and empower local communities to develop their own projects. If you are a member of ABCD in Action, you can download this tool kit at http://abcdinaction .org/forum/download/forum_file/1048/ABCD%20 Toolkit.pdf.

A Guide to Capacity Inventories: Mobilizing the Community Skills of Local Residents. A community-building workbook from the Asset-Based Community Development Institute, Institute for Policy Research, 2040 Sheridan Road, Evanston, Illinois 60208-4100; http://communitymagic.org/public/A%20Guide %20to%20Capacity%20Inventories.pdf. This guide was developed to report how a number of community groups used an asset-based approach in their community-building efforts, and how they developed and implemented a capacity inventory project through which they identified and mobilized the gifts and skills of local people. The asset-based community-building approach illustrated in this guide was developed by John McKnight and John Kretzmann and presented in their manual *Building Communities from the Inside Out.* While that book contains a single example of an individual capacity inventory, this guide introduces a much wider variety of inventories, used in different kinds of communities for many different community-building purposes.

Stuart, Graeme, Family Action Centre, University of Newcastle, Callaghan NSW 2308. Australia has a reading list on ABCD with over one hundred resources from around the globe posted on the Sustaining Community website: https://sustainingcommunity.wordpress .com/2016/04/11/abcd-reading-list/#start.

ABCD WEB COMMUNITIES AND INSTITUTES

The **Asset-Based Community Development Institute
(ABCD)** is at the center of a large and growing movement
that considers local assets as the primary building blocks
of sustainable community development. Building on the
skills of local residents, the power of local associations, and
the supportive functions of local institutions, asset-based
community development draws upon existing community
strengths to build stronger, more sustainable communities
for the future. https://resources.depaul.edu/abcd-institute
/Pages/default.aspx.

ABCD in Action is a community of members from
around the world who explore together how to apply the
principles and practices of asset-based community development (ABCD). This site is hosted by the ABCD Institute; www.abcdinaction.org.

NOTES

INTRODUCTION

1. Jose Marins, conversations with Rob Mueller.
2. Shane Claiborne, *The Irresistible Revolution: Living as an Ordinary Radical* (Grand Rapids: Zondervan, 2006), 89.
3. Paulo Freire, *Pedagogy of the Oppressed, 30th Anniversary Edition* (New York: Bloomsbury, 2000), 178.
4. Robert Ludlum, *Toxic Charity: How Churches and Charities Hurt Those They Help (And How to Reverse It)* (New York: Harper Collins, 2011), 4.

CHAPTER 1: COMMUNAL CONVERSION

1. James Fowler, *Stages of Faith, The Psychology of Human Development and the Quest for Meaning* (San Francisco: Harper and Row, 1981), 31.
2. *Twelve Steps and Twelve Traditions* (New York: Alcoholics Anonymous World Services, 1981), 95.
3. Robert Schnase, *Five Practices of Fruitful Congregations* (Nashville: Abingdon Press, 2018), 133.
4. Erica Schemper, www.reformedworship.org/article/june -2014/abundance-god.

5. Walter Bruggemann, "The Myth of Scarcity, the Liturgy of Abundance," *Christian Century*, March 24, 1999.

6. Richard Rohr, *Falling Upward: A Spirituality for the Two Halves of Life* (San Francisco: Jossey-Bass, 2011), 151.

7. George Hunter, *Radical Outreach: The Recovery of Apostolic Ministry and Evangelism* (Nashville: Abingdon Press, 2003), 187.

8. Robert King, "Death and Resurrection of an Urban Church," *Faith and Leadership*, March 2015.

9. "Who We Are," Broadway United Methodist Church, www.broadwayumc.org/who-we-are/.

CHAPTER 2: THE DNA OF LISTENING

1. Kay Lindahl, quoted from the website of the Learning Center, www.sacredlistening.com.

2. Dave Isay, *Listening Is an Act of Love: A Celebration of American Life from the StoryCorps Project* (New York: Penguin Press, 2007), 1.

3. *Dare to Listen*, idaretolisten.org.

4. Adam S. McHugh, *The Listening Life: Embracing Attentiveness in a World of Distraction* (Downer's Grove, IL: InterVarsity Press, 2016), 100.

CHAPTER 3: TRANSFORMING PARTNERSHIP

1. Walter Bruggemann, *Genesis*, Interpretation (Atlanta: John Knox Press, 1982), 171–73.

2. Sherron George, *Called as Partners in Christ's Service: The Practice of God's Mission* (Louisville, KY: Geneva Press, 2004).

3. Micky ScottBey Jones, "Invitation to Brave Space," http://www.mickyscottbeyjones.com/invitation-to-brave-space/.

CHAPTER 4: INTEGRATING OUR SPACE

1. Jules Loh, *Lords of the Earth: A History of the Navajo Indians* (New York: Crowell-Collier, 1971), 51.
2. Tim Cool, *Why Church Buildings Matter* (Nashville: Ranier Publishing, 2016), 9.
3. Partners for Sacred Places, *Three City Arts Study*, http://sacredplaces.org/tools-research/3-city-arts-study.

CHAPTER 5: SUSTAINING THE VISION

1. Edwin Friedman, *A Failure of Nerve: Leadership in the Age of the Quick Fix* (New York: Church Publishing, 1999), 14.
2. Paul Seebeck, "Faith and Sports," *Presbyterians Today*, February/March 2018, 28.
3. Robert Schnase, *Five Practices of Fruitful Congregations* (Nashville: Abingdon Press, 2018), 52.
4. Tony Campolo, *Wake Up, America! Answering God's Radical Call While Living in the Real World* (Grand Rapids: Zondervan, 1991), 7.
5. Robert Schnase, *Five Practices of Fruitful Congregations,* (Nashville: Abingdon Press, 2007), 42.
6. John Paul II, speech given to participants in the National Congress of the Ecclesial Movement for Cultural Commitment, Rome, 1982.
7. Barbara A. Holmes, *Joy Unspeakable: Contemplative Practices of the Black Church*, 2nd ed. (Minneapolis: Fortress Press, 2017), 183–85.
8. Jose Marins, conversations with Rob Mueller.
9. *Book of Common Worship* (Louisville: KY: Westminster John Knox Press, 2018), 409.
10. E. Stanley Ott, *The Joy of Discipling: Friend with Friend, Heart with Heart* (Grand Rapids: Lamplighter Books, 1989), 36–37.

11. Henri J.M. Nouwen, *Bread for the Journey: A Daybook of Wisdom and Faith* (New York: HarperCollins, 1997), July 8 entry.

CONCLUSION

1. J. Herbert Nelson, "Overcoming Our Fear of Transformative Change in the PC(USA)," http://www.pcusa.org/news/2018/3/13/overcoming-our-fear-transformative-change-pcusa/.

2. Partners for Sacred Places, *Economic Halo Effect of Sacred Places,* http://sacredplaces.org/tools-research/halo-effect.

CPSIA information can be obtained
at www.ICGtesting.com
Printed in the USA
FFHW011642030219
50391994-55537FF